EDITORIAL STAFF

Vice President and Editor-in-Chief: Sandra Graham Case. *Executive Director of Publications:* Cheryl Nodine Gunnells. *Director of Designer Relations:* Debra Nettles. *Senior Publications Director:* Susan White Sullivan. *Editorial Director:* Susan Frantz Wiles. *Art Operations Director:* Jeff Curtis. *Director of Public Relations and Retail Marketing:* Stephen Wilson. PRODUCTION — *Leaflet Publications Director:* Mary Sullivan Hutcheson. *Senior Technical Editor:* Carolyn Breeding. *Assistant Technical Editors:* Mimi Harrington, Karen Jackson, and Merrilee Gasaway. *Production Assistants:* Karla Edgar and Kathy Elrod. EDITORIAL — *Associate Editors:* Kimberly L. Ross and Susan McManus Johnson. ART — *Art Publications Director:* Rhonda Hodge Shelby. *Art Imaging Director:* Mark Hawkins. *Senior Graphic Artist:* Chaska Richardson Lucas. *Lead Graphic Artist:* Karen F. Allbright. *Graphic Artist:* Shalana Fleetwood. *Photography Stylist:* Janna B. Laughlin. *Staff Photographer:* Russell Ganser. *Publishing Systems Administrator:* Becky Riddle. *Publishing Systems Assistants:* Clint Hanson, John Rose, and Chris Wertenberger.

BUSINESS STAFF

Publisher: Rick Barton. *Vice President, Finance:* Tom Siebenmorgen. *Director of Corporate Planning and Development:* Laticia Mull Dittrich. *Vice President, Retail Marketing:* Bob Humphrey. *Vice President, Sales:* Ray Shelgosh. *Vice President, National Accounts:* Pam Stebbins. *Director of Sales and Services:* Margaret Reinold. *Vice President, Operations:* Jim Dittrich. *Comptroller, Operations:* Rob Thieme. *Retail Customer Service Manager:* Stan Raynor. *Print Production Manager:* Fred F. Pruss.

Known for her natural style and variety of interests, **Cathy Livingston** will forever be remembered as one of the cross stitch world's most treasured designers. And now, for the first time in years, this delightful collection offers you a chance to enjoy anew **20 of her most cherished patterns**. From traditional samplers and portraits of Nature to sensitive depictions of the animal kingdom, these classic designs demonstrate Cathy's extraordinary gift to beautifully illustrate an array of subjects. So gather your needle and floss and **prepare to be enchanted** by the cross stitch artistry of Cathy Livingston.

A LEISURE ARTS PUBLICATION

A special thanks goes to our friends at Just CrossStitch® magazine for the information used in writing Cathy Livingston's biography.

Made in the United States of America.

Softcover ISBN 1-57486-373-8

10 9 8 7 6 5 4 3 2 1

Throughout her life, **Cathy Livingston** had two great passions: art and nature. Her childhood love of painting led her to study at the University of Tennessee, Knoxville, where she majored in watercolors and received a B.A. of Fine Arts with honors.

After graduating, Cathy spent time working for the university's department of animal science. She soon developed an interest in depicting some of the farm animals kept there.

In the late 1970's, Cathy discovered needlework, beginning with kits of crewel embroidery and surface embroidery techniques. Eventually, a friend taught Cathy to work counted cross stitch. Her first project was a collection of ornaments on Hardanger.

> # A great designer in every sense of the word...

It didn't take long for Cathy to begin designing for her new pastime. "Why should I buy patterns when I can draw them myself?" she reasoned. A friend bolstered Cathy's inclination by daring her to design something on the spot. She rose to the challenge by drafting a small dogwood, and she never looked back.

For several years Cathy designed commissioned work based on photographs. Then, in 1988, she became a nationally published artist when *Just CrossStitch*® magazine accepted her design *Madonna with Christ Child*. That same year, Cathy began working as a staff designer for Symbol of Excellence Publishers, Inc., where she continued to work until her death in 1994.

A great designer in every sense of the word, Cathy excelled at designing a wide variety of themes, although birds and animals were her preferred models. In fact, one of her favorite designs, an African elephant, is included on page 10 of this book. But whatever her subject, Cathy always strove to **"paint with a needle and thread."** Without a doubt, she succeeded.

Table Of Contents

Pear 4
     chart on page 16
Apple 4
     chart on page 18
Fruit Tapestry 5
     chart on page 20
Floral Tapestry Circle 6
     chart on page 24
Floral Tapestry Square 6
     chart on page 28
Caladiums 7
     chart on page 64
Water Lilies 7
     chart on page 68
Cheetah 8
     chart on page 38
Lion Family 9
     chart on page 44
Giraffe 10
     chart on page 50
Elephant 10
     chart on page 54
Zebra 10
     chart on page 58
Tiger 11
     chart on page 32
Spring in Bloom 12
     chart on page 72
Summer Garden 12
     chart on page 74
Fall Harvesttime 12
     chart on page 76
Wintertime 12
     chart on page 78
Flora Sampler 13
     chart on page 80
Remember Me Sampler 14
     chart on page 86
Saw-Whet Owls 15
     chart on page 92
General Instructions 95

4

14

PEARS

X	DMC	ANC.
△	*310 & 500	403 & 683
○	*402 & 834	1047 & 874
C	433	358
−	434	310
V	469	267
L	470	267
✕	†471	266
H	★500	683
◇	*712 & 727	926 & 293
✳	*725 & 833	305 & 907
6	*727 & 834	293 & 874
◢	*782 & 830	307 & 277
5	*783 & 832	306 & 907
+	*833 & 3777	907 & 1015
n	898	360
T	†936	269
3	†937	268

Grey area indicates last row
of previous section of design.

* Use **2** strands of each floss color listed.

† You will need **2** skeins of floss.

★ You will need **4** skeins of floss.

Design was stitched on an 18" x 18" piece
of 18 count Clay Cork Linen (design size
11⅞" x 11⅞") over two fabric threads.
Four strands of floss were used for Cross
Stitch. It was made into a pillow. See
Making a Pillow, pg. 96.

Stitch Count (106w x 106h)

14 count	7⅝"	x	7⅝"
16 count	6⅝"	x	6⅝"
18 count	6"	x	6"

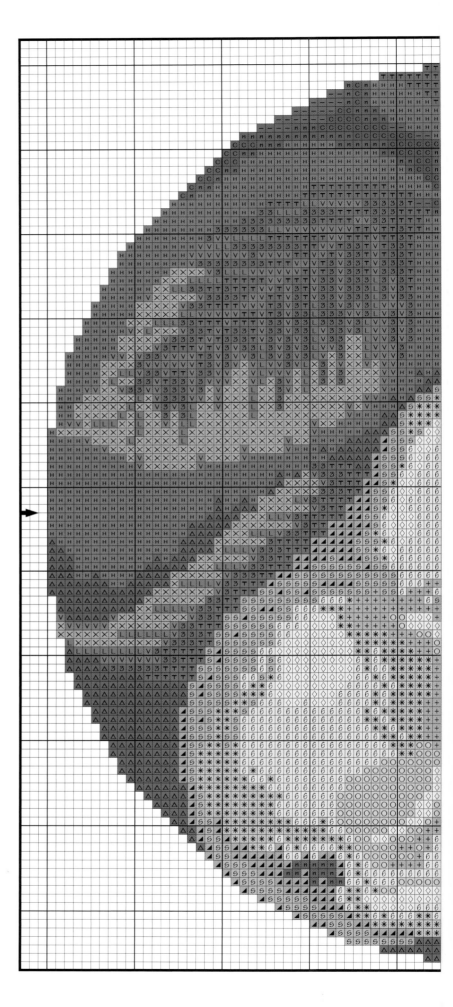

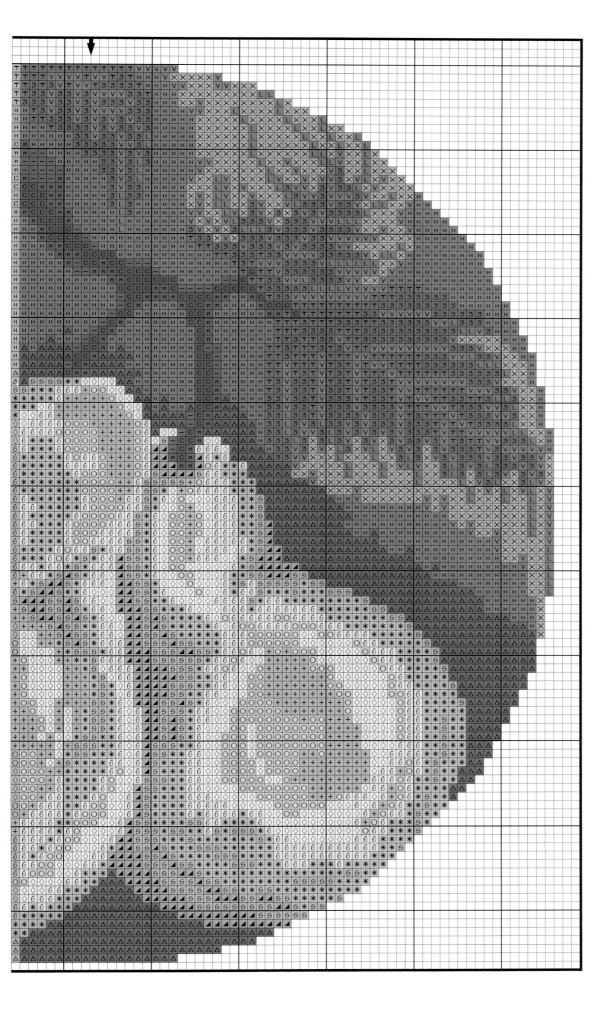

WINESAP APPLES

X	DMC	ANC.
2	*310 & 500	403 & 683
a	*349 & 921	13 & 1003
✳	*350 & 900	11 & 333
C	433	358
−	434	310
V	469	267
L	470	267
e	*470 & 721	267 & 925
X	†471	266
+	*471 & 725	266 & 305
S	*472 & 726	253 & 295
▲	★500	683
>	*727 & 746	293 & 275
⊥	*817 & 918	13 & 341
n	898	360
T	†936	269
3	†937	268

Grey area indicates last row of previous section of design.

* Use **2** strands of each floss color listed.

† You will need **2** skeins of floss.

★ You will need **4** skeins of floss.

Design was stitched on an 18" x 18" piece of 18 count Clay Cork Linen (design size 11⅞" x 11⅞") over two fabric threads. Four strands of floss were used for Cross Stitch. It was made into a pillow. See Making a Pillow, pg. 96.

Stitch Count (106w x 106h)

14 count	7⅝"	x	7⅝"
16 count	6⅝"	x	6⅝"
18 count	6"	x	6"

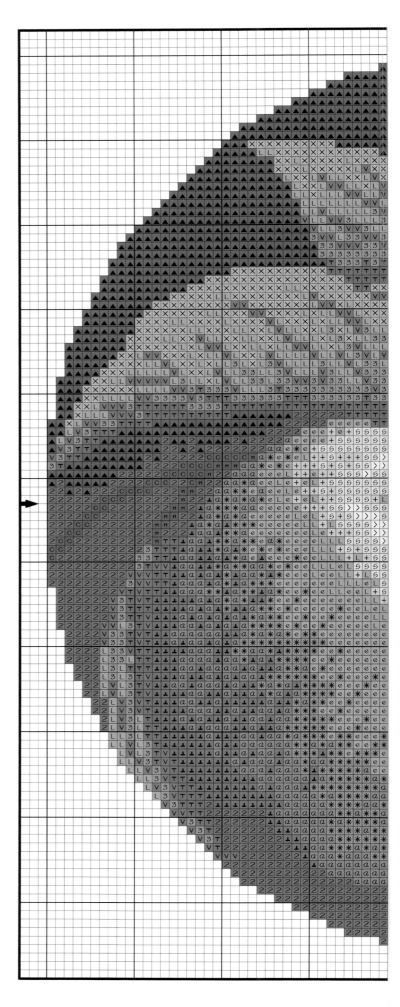

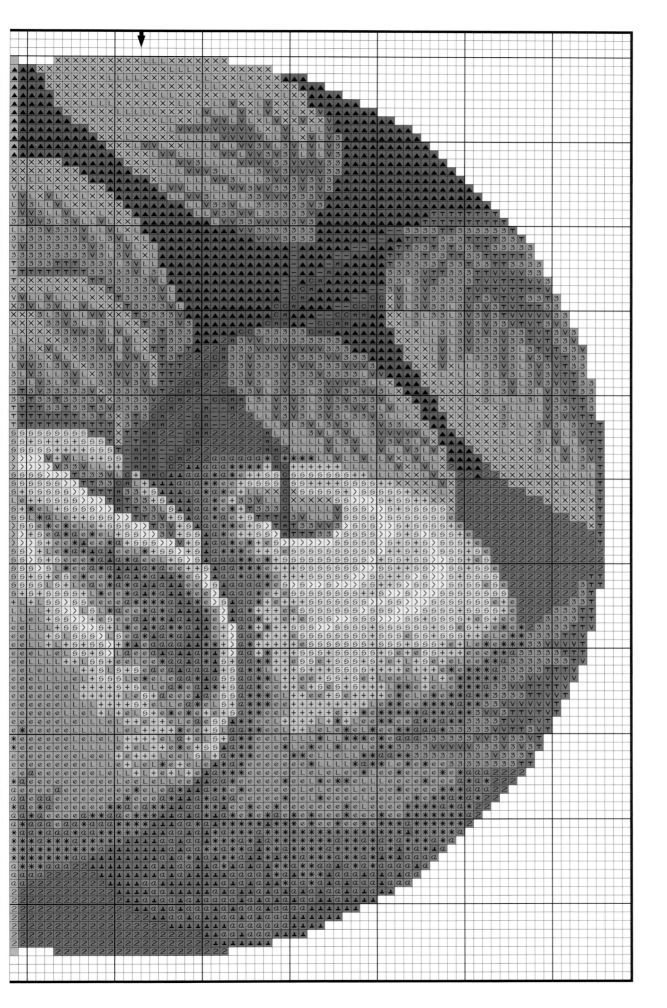

19

FRUIT TAPESTRY

X	DMC	ANC.
✚	*304	1006
4	309	42
★	420	374
✳	422	943
m	433	358
V	*469	267
=	*471	266
L	550	102
e	552	99
>	553	98
2	554	96
○	677	886

X	DMC	ANC.
8	*720	326
C	*721	925
L	722	323
⊥	729	890
◢	732	281
a	733	280
✓	734	279
−	746	275
6	*814	45
▲	*815	43
Z	816	1005
╱	823	152

X	DMC	ANC.
▲	898	360
⬤	902	897
H	930	1035
△	931	1034
✕	*935	861
3	*936	269
n	3051	681
I	*3052	262

Grey area indicates last row
of previous section of design.

* You will need **2** skeins of floss.

Section 1

Design was stitched on a 22" x 20" piece of 20 count Cream Irish Linen (design size 16" x 14") over two fabric threads. Four strands of floss were used for Cross Stitch. It was made into a pillow. See Making a Pillow, pg. 96.

Stitch Count (160w x 140h)

14 count	11½"	x	10"
16 count	10"	x	8¾"
18 count	9"	x	7⅞"

Chart sections are on pgs. 20-23.
See placement diagram below.

Section 1	Section 2
Section 3	Section 4

Section 2

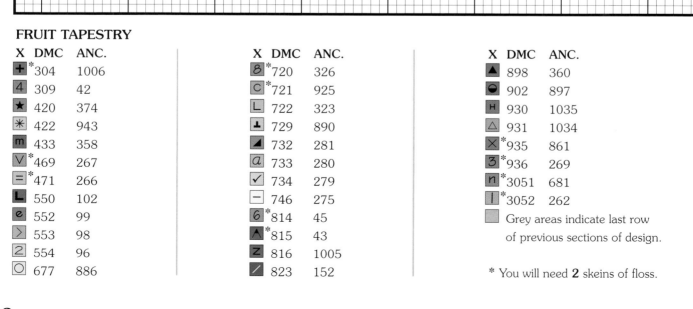

FRUIT TAPESTRY

X	DMC	ANC.
+	*304	1006
4	309	42
★	420	374
*	422	943
m	433	358
V	*469	267
=	*471	266
L	550	102
e	552	99
>	553	98
2	554	96
O	677	886

X	DMC	ANC.
8	*720	326
C	*721	925
L	722	323
⊥	729	890
◢	732	281
a	733	280
✓	734	279
−	746	275
6	*814	45
▲	*815	43
Z	816	1005
╱	823	152

X	DMC	ANC.
▲	898	360
◐	902	897
H	930	1035
△	931	1034
X	*935	861
3	*936	269
n	*3051	681
I	*3052	262

Grey areas indicate last row of previous sections of design.

* You will need **2** skeins of floss.

FLORAL TAPESTRY CIRCLE

X	DMC	ANC.
a	347	1025
6	349	13
I	350	11
e	351	10
V	352	9
−	353	6
◢	433	358
n	725	305
S	726	295
◇	727	293

X	DMC	ANC.
C	744	301
I	745	300
2	746	275
L	754	1012
∧	760	1022
¢	761	1021
3	781	308
+	783	306
△ *895		1044
Z	926	850

X	DMC	ANC.
T	927	848
∩	928	274
m	930	1035
>	931	1034
H	932	1033
□	948	1011
*	3328	1024
X †3345		268
O *3346		267
/	3347	266

X	DMC	ANC.
◌	3712	1023
~	3713	1020

Grey area indicates last row
of previous section of design.

* You will need **2** skeins of floss.

† You will need **3** skeins of floss.

Section 1

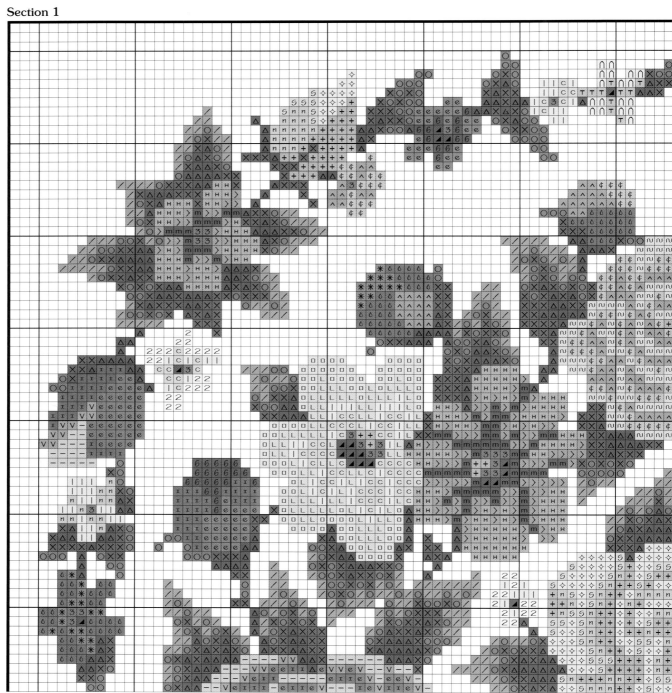

24

Design was stitched on a 17" x 17 ½" piece of 25 count Black Lugana (design size 9 ⅝" x 10") over two fabric threads. Three strands of floss were used for Cross Stitch. It was made into a pillow. See Making a Pillow, pg. 96.

Stitch Count (134w x 140h)

14 count	9 ⅝"	x	10"
16 count	8 ⅜"	x	8 ¾"
18 count	7 ½"	x	7 ⅞"

Chart sections are on pgs. 24-27.
See placement diagram below.

Section 1	Section 2
Section 3	Section 4

Section 2

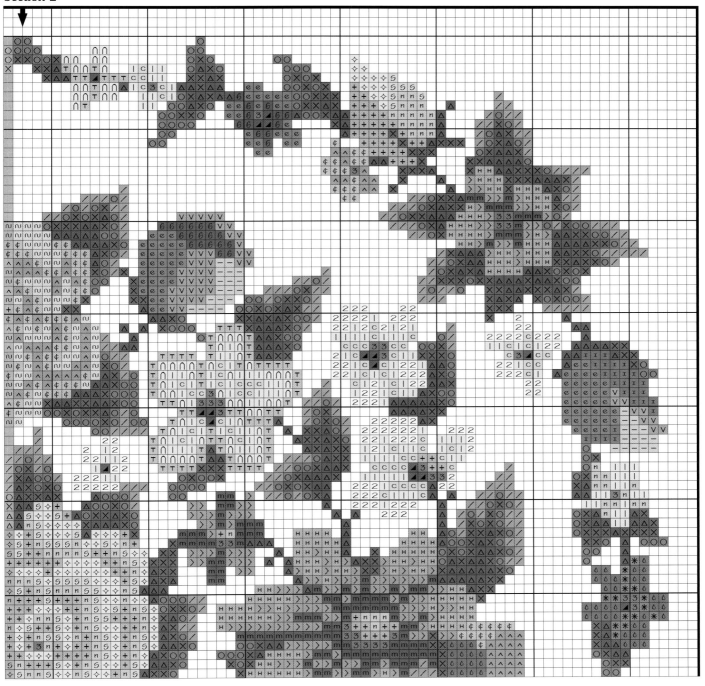

FLORAL TAPESTRY CIRCLE

X	DMC	ANC.	X	DMC	ANC.	X	DMC	ANC.	X	DMC	ANC.
a	347	1025	c	744	301	T	927	848	◖	3712	1023
6	349	13	I	745	300	∩	928	274	∾	3713	1020
I	350	11	2	746	275	m	930	1035			
e	351	10	L	754	1012	>	931	1034			
V	352	9	∧	760	1022	H	932	1033			
−	353	6	¢	761	1021	□	948	1011			
◢	433	358	3	781	308	✳	3328	1024			
n	725	305	+	783	306	X †3345		268			
S	726	295	△ *895		1044	O *3346		267			
◇	727	293	Z	926	850	╱	3347	266			

Grey areas indicate last row
of previous sections of design.

* You will need **2** skeins of floss.

† You will need **3** skeins of floss.

FLORAL TAPESTRY SQUARE

X	DMC	ANC.
𝕊	309	42
√	326	59
∩	335	38
a	347	1025
6	349	13
I	350	11
V	352	9
−	353	6
n	725	305
C	744	301

X	DMC	ANC.
l	745	300
2	746	275
L	754	1012
∧	760	1022
¢	761	1021
3	781	308
+	783	306
△*	895	1044
T	927	848
∩	928	274
m	930	1035

X	DMC	ANC.
>	931	1034
H	932	1033
□	948	1011
✳	3328	1024
✕*	3345	268
○*	3346	267
╱	3347	266

Grey area indicates last row
of previous section of design.

* You will need **2** skeins of floss.

Section 1

28

Design was stitched on an 18" x 17" piece of 25 count Black Lugana (design size 12" x 11") over two fabric threads. Three strands of floss were used for Cross Stitch. It was made into a pillow. See Making a Pillow, pg. 96.

Stitch Count (150w x 136h)

14 count	10¾" x 9¾"	
16 count	9⅜" x 8½"	
18 count	8⅜" x 7⅝"	

Chart sections are on pgs. 28-31.
See placement diagram below.

Section 1	Section 2
Section 3	Section 4

Section 2

FLORAL TAPESTRY SQUARE

X	DMC	ANC.
5	309	42
√	326	59
∩	335	38
a	347	1025
6	349	13
I	350	11
V	352	9
−	353	6
n	725	305
C	744	301
I	745	300

X	DMC	ANC.
2	746	275
L	754	1012
∧	760	1022
¢	761	1021
3	781	308
+	783	306
△*	895	1044
T	927	848
∩	928	274
m	930	1035
>	931	1034

X	DMC	ANC.
H	932	1033
□	948	1011
*	3328	1024
X*	3345	268
O*	3346	267
/	3347	266

Grey areas indicate last row
of previous sections of design.

* You will need **2** skeins of floss.

TIGER

X	DMC	¼X	B'ST	ANC.
☆	blanc		/†	2
••	*blanc & 301	••		2 & 1049
n	*blanc & 310	n		2 & 403
/	*blanc & 402	/		2 & 1047
△	*blanc & 414	△		2 & 235
✓	*blanc & 415	✓		2 & 398
◤	300	◤		352
L	*300 & 310	L		352 & 403
❯	301	❯		1049

X	DMC	¼X	B'ST	ANC.
m	*301 & 310	m		1049 & 403
◆	*301 & 414	◆		1049 & 235
¢	*301 & 975	c		1049 & 355
+	*301 & 3776	+		1049 & 1048
(	310	(	/	403
❮	312	❮		979
◣	*312 & 935	◣		979 & 861
⌃	*312 & 937	⌃		979 & 268
	355 & 356	↗*		1014 & 5975

X	DMC	¼X	ANC.
★	*356 & 413	★	5975 & 236
8	*356 & 414		5975 & 235
◓	*356 & 3778		5975 & 1013
e	*402 & 414		1047 & 235
5	*402 & 415	5	1047 & 398
a	*402 & 3776	a	1047 & 1048
C	*415 & 758	c	398 & 868
⊘	470	ø	267

Section 1

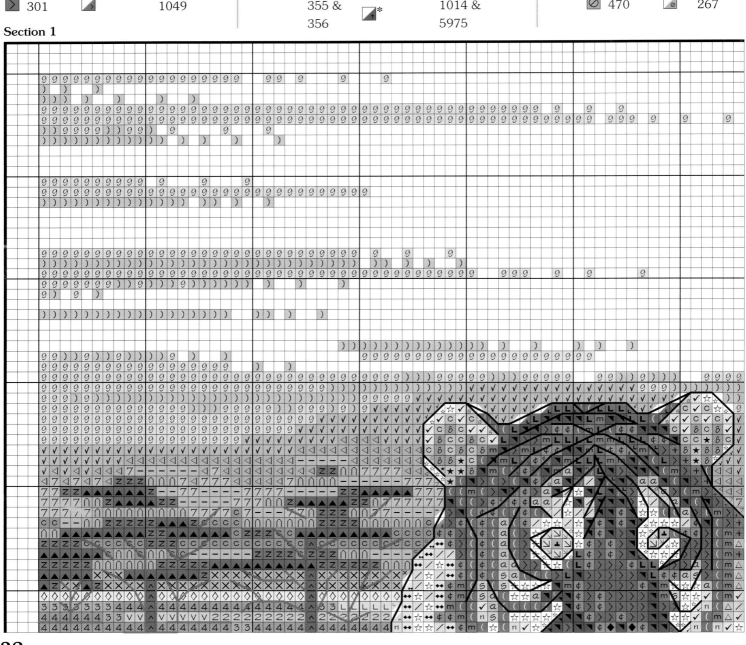

32

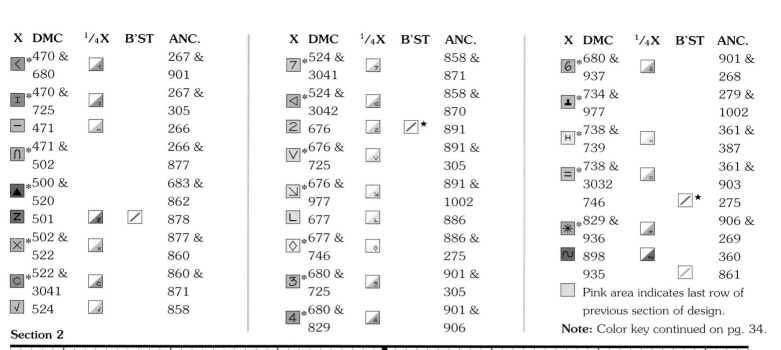

X DMC	¹/₄X	B'ST	ANC.	X DMC	¹/₄X	B'ST	ANC.	X DMC	¹/₄X	B'ST	ANC.
*470 & 680			267 & 901	7 *524 & 3041			858 & 871	6 *680 & 937			901 & 268
I *470 & 725			267 & 305	◁ *524 & 3042			858 & 870	⊥ *734 & 977			279 & 1002
− 471			266	2 676		╱★	891	H *738 & 739			361 & 387
∩ *471 & 502			266 & 877	V *676 & 725			891 & 305	= *738 & 3032			361 & 903
▲ *500 & 520			683 & 862	↘ *676 & 977			891 & 1002	746		╱★	275
Z 501		╱	878	L 677			886	* *829 & 936			906 & 269
X *502 & 522			877 & 860	◇ *677 & 746			886 & 275	∪ 898			360
C *522 & 3041			860 & 871	3 *680 & 725			901 & 305	935		╱	861
√ 524			858	4 *680 & 829			901 & 906				

Pink area indicates last row of previous section of design.

Note: Color key continued on pg. 34.

Section 2

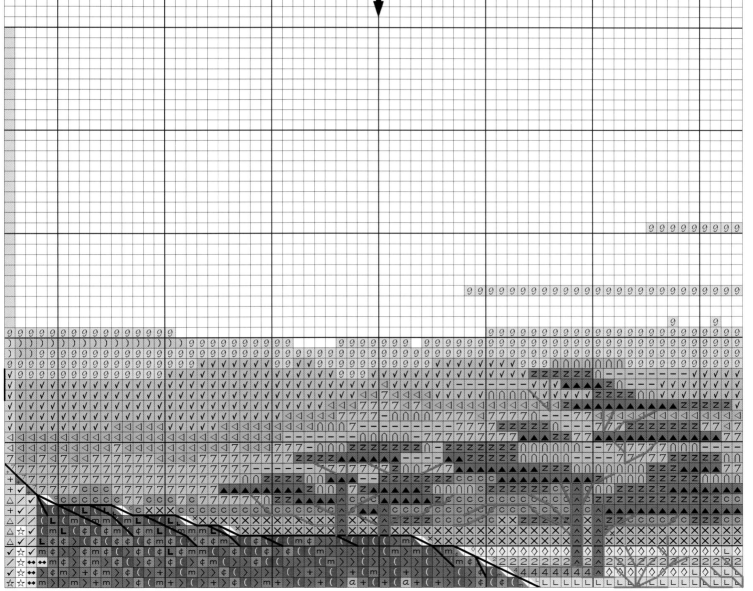

TIGER

X	DMC	¼X	½X	B'ST	ANC.
5	937	5		✎★	268
	3031			✎	905
◣	3032	◣			903
	3743		)		869
	3752		9		1032
T	3778				1013
∧	3781	∧			904

☐ Pink area indicates last row of previous section of design.

* Use **1** strand of each floss color listed.

† Use long stitches.

★ Use long stitches and randomly place colors when stitching grass.

Design was stitched on a 20½" x 14" piece of 28 count Sandstone Linen (design size 14⅜" x 7⅞") over two fabric threads. Two strands of floss were used for Cross Stitch and Half Cross Stitches and 1 strand for Backstitch. It was custom framed.

Stitch Count (200w x 110h)

14 count	14⅜" x 7⅞"	
16 count	12½" x 6⅞"	
18 count	11⅛" x 6⅛"	

Chart sections are on pgs. 32-37. See placement diagram below.

Section 1	Section 2	Section 3
Section 4	Section 5	Section 6

Section 3

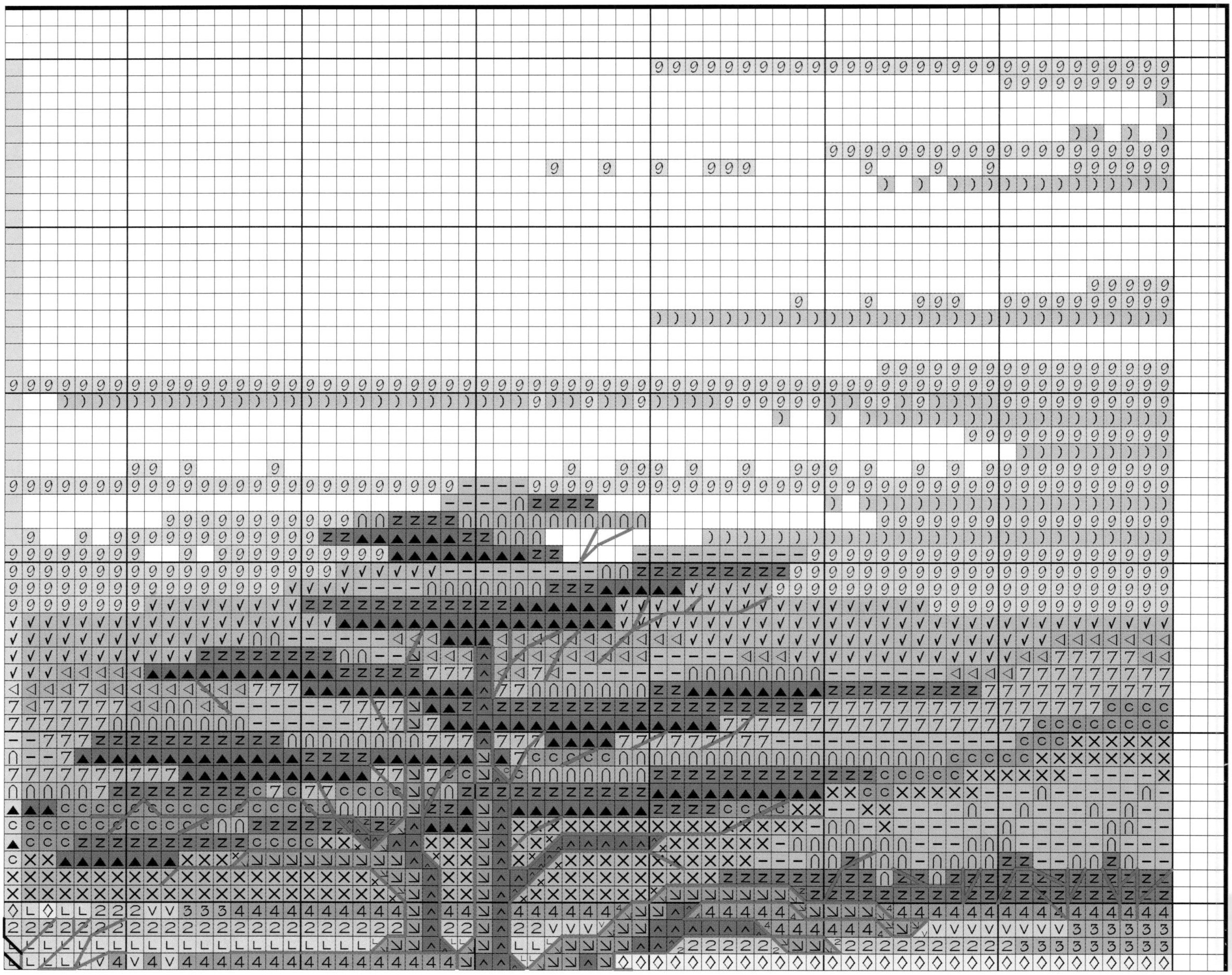

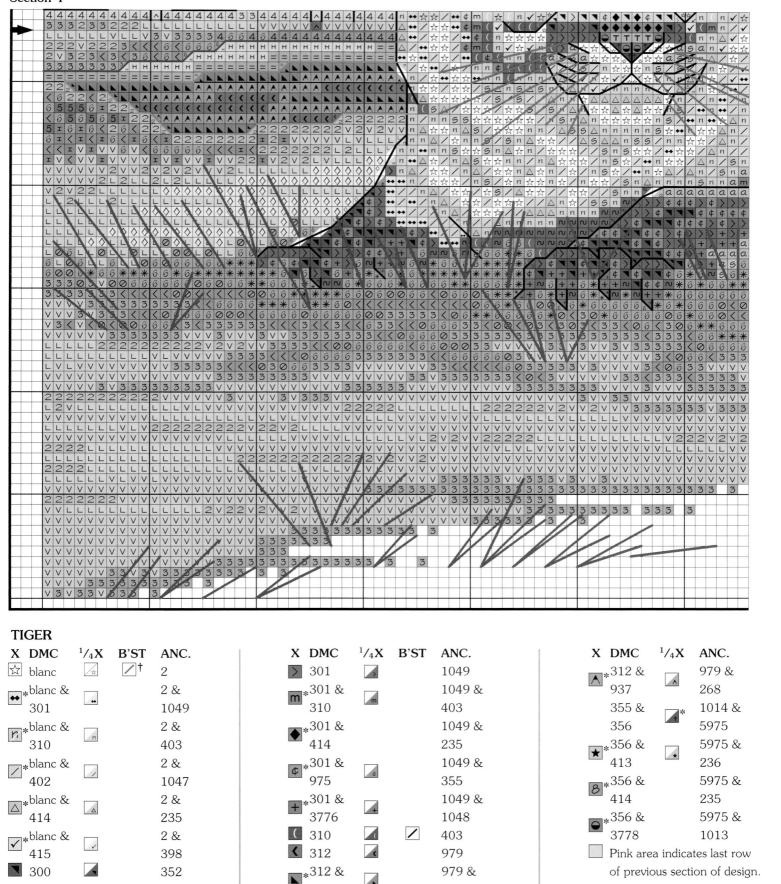

TIGER

X	DMC	¼X	B'ST	ANC.
☆	blanc		⁄†	2
✦	blanc & 301			2 & 1049
n*	blanc & 310			2 & 403
⁄*	blanc & 402			2 & 1047
△*	blanc & 414			2 & 235
✓*	blanc & 415			2 & 398
◣	300			352
L*	300 & 310			352 & 403

X	DMC	¼X	B'ST	ANC.
▶	301			1049
m*	301 & 310			1049 & 403
◆*	301 & 414			1049 & 235
¢*	301 & 975			1049 & 355
+*	301 & 3776			1049 & 1048
◖	310		⁄	403
◀	312			979
◣*	312 & 935			979 & 861

X	DMC	¼X	ANC.
▲*	312 & 937		979 & 268
	355 & 356	◢*	1014 & 5975
★*	356 & 413		5975 & 236
8*	356 & 414		5975 & 235
⊖*	356 & 3778		5975 & 1013
☐	Pink area indicates last row of previous section of design.

Note: Color key continued on pgs. 36 and 37.

TIGER

X	DMC	1/4X	ANC.
e*	402 & 414		1047 & 235
S*	402 & 415	S	1047 & 398
a*	402 & 3776	a	1047 & 1048
C*	415 & 758	C	398 & 868
⊘	470	⊘	267
<*	470 & 680	<	267 & 901
I*	470 & 725	I	267 & 305
–	471	–	266

X	DMC	1/4X	B'ST	ANC.
∩*	471 & 502			266 & 877
▲*	500 & 520			683 & 862
Z	501	Z	/	878
X*	502 & 522	X		877 & 860
C*	522 & 3041	C		860 & 871
√	524	√		858
7*	524 & 3041	7		858 & 871
◁*	524 & 3042	◁		858 & 870

X	DMC	1/4X	B'ST	ANC.
2	676	2	/★	891
V*	676 & 725	V		891 & 305
↘*	676 & 977	↘		891 & 1002
L	677	L		886
◇*	677 & 746	◇		886 & 275
3*	680 & 725	3		901 & 305
4*	680 & 829	4		901 & 906
6*	680 & 937	6		901 & 268

X	DMC	¼X	B'ST	ANC.
⊥	*734 &			279 &
	977			1002
H	*738 &	H		361 &
	739			387
=	*738 &	=		361 &
	3032			903
	746		/★	275
*	*829 &	*		906 &
	936			269
~	898	~		360
	935		/	861
5	937	5	/★	268
	3031		/	905
⊿	3032	⊿		903

X	DMC	¼X	½X	ANC.
	3743		)	869
	3752		9	1032
T	3778			1013
∧	3781	◿		904

Pink areas indicate last row of previous sections of design.

* Use **1** strand of each floss color listed.
† Use long stitches.
★ Use long stitches and randomly place colors when stitching grass.

CHEETAH

X	DMC	¼X	B'ST	ANC.
☆	blanc	☆	/†	2
e	*blanc & 310	e		2 & 403
#	*blanc & 437	#		2 & 362
8	ecru	8		387
a	*ecru & 739	a		387 & 387
n	*300 & 301	n		352 & 1049
∧	*301 & 3012	∧		1049 & 844
)	310	)	/★	403
◊	*372 & 647	◊		853 & 1040

X	DMC	¼X	B'ST	ANC.
⊥	435	⊥		1046
✓	*435 & 3781	✓		1046 & 904
2	436	2	/†	1045
+	*437 & 738	+		362 & 361
m	*470 & 680	m		267 & 901
$	471	$		266
♡	*471 & 502	♡		266 & 877
▲	*500 & 520	▲		683 & 862
z	501	z	/†	878
✗	*502 & 522	✗		877 & 860

X	DMC	¼X	B'ST	ANC.
C	*522 & 3041	c		860 & 871
∩	*524 & 3743	∩		858 & 869
>	*613 & 648	>		831 & 900
↑	645	↑		273
6	*645 & 3012	6		273 & 844
S	647	s		1040
−	648	−		900
L	676	L	/+	891
★	*676 & 725	★		891 & 305
7	*677 & 746	7		886 & 275

Section 1

X	DMC	¼X	B'ST	ANC.		X	DMC	¼X	½X	B'ST	ANC.
	680		╱+	901		▼	*844 &		✓		1041 &
3	*680 &	3		901 &			3371				382
	725			305		⋈	936				269
L	*680 &	L		901 &		5	3021	5		╱★	905
	937			268		▲	3041	▲			871
4	738	4		361		=	*3041 &	=			871 &
¢	*738 &	¢		361 &			3042				870 &
	3782			899		▼	3371	▼			382
◇	739	◇		387			3743		⌐		869
T	*739 &	T		387 &			3752		╱		1032
	3033			391		●	310 Fr. Knot				403
H	*829 &	H		906 &							
	936			269			Pink area indicates last row of previous				
	937		╱+	268			section of design.				
✳	844	✳	╱	1041							

*Use **1** strand of each floss color listed.

† **DMC blanc** for whiskers. **DMC 436** for mouth and right side of cheetah. **DMC 501** for horizon.

★ **DMC 310** for cheetah (use **2** strands for each side of nose below eyes). **DMC 3021** for trees.

+ Use long stitches and randomly place colors when stitching grass.

Design was stitched on a 21½" x 14½" piece of 26 count White Birch Heatherfield (design size 15½" x 8½") over two fabric threads. Two strands of floss were used for Cross Stitch, Half Cross Stitches, and French Knots and 1 strand for Backstitch except where noted in key. It was custom framed.

Section 2

Stitch Count (200w x 110h)	
14 count	14³⁄₈" x 7⁷⁄₈"
16 count	12½" x 6⁷⁄₈"
18 count	11¹⁄₈" x 6¹⁄₈"

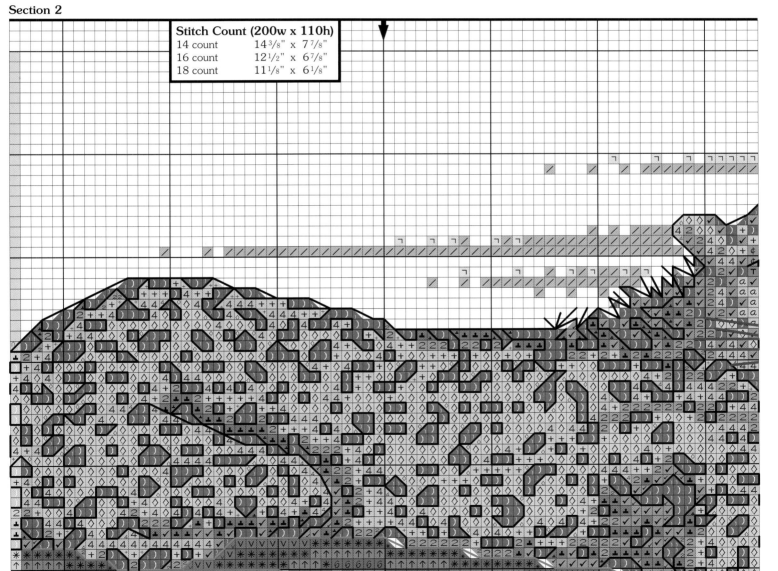

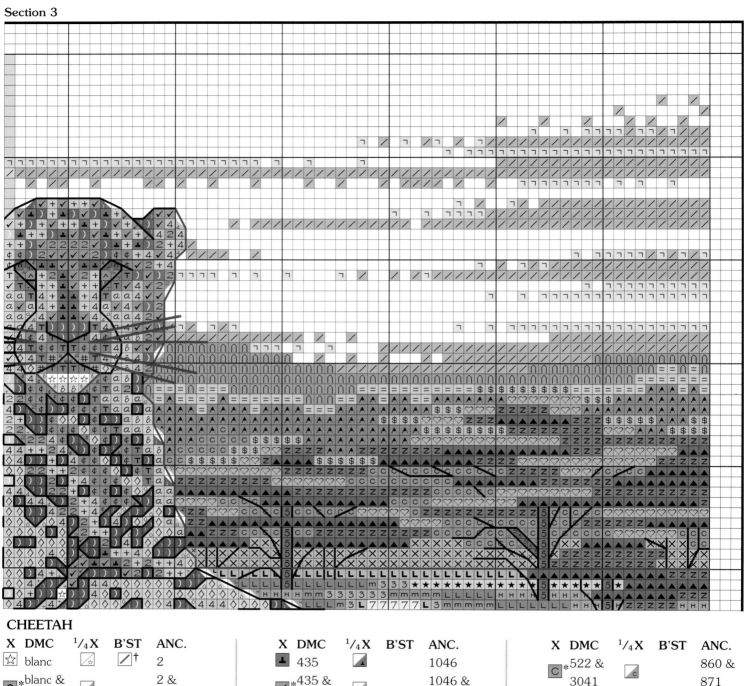

CHEETAH

X	DMC	¼X	B'ST	ANC.
☆	blanc		⁄†	2
e	*blanc & 310	e		2 & 403
#	*blanc & 437	#		2 & 362
ठ	ecru	ठ		387
a	*ecru & 739	a		387 & 387
n	*300 & 301	n		352 & 1049
∧	*301 & 3012	∧		1049 & 844
)	310	)	⁄★	403
◊	*372 & 647	◊		853 & 1040

X	DMC	¼X	B'ST	ANC.
⬓	435			1046
✓	*435 & 3781			1046 & 904
2	436	2	⁄†	1045
+	*437 & 738	+		362 & 361
m	*470 & 680	m		267 & 901
$	471	$		266
♡	*471 & 502	♡		266 & 877
▲	*500 & 520	▲		683 & 862
Z	501	z	⁄†	878
✕	*502 & 522	✕		877 & 860

X	DMC	¼X	B'ST	ANC.
C	*522 & 3041	c		860 & 871
∩	*524 & 3743	∩		858 & 869
>	*613 & 648	>		831 & 900
↑	645	↑		273
6	*645 & 3012	6		273 & 844
5	647	5		1040
−	648	−		900
L	676	L	⁄+	891
★	*676 & 725	★		891 & 305
7	*677 & 746	7		886 & 275

Section 4

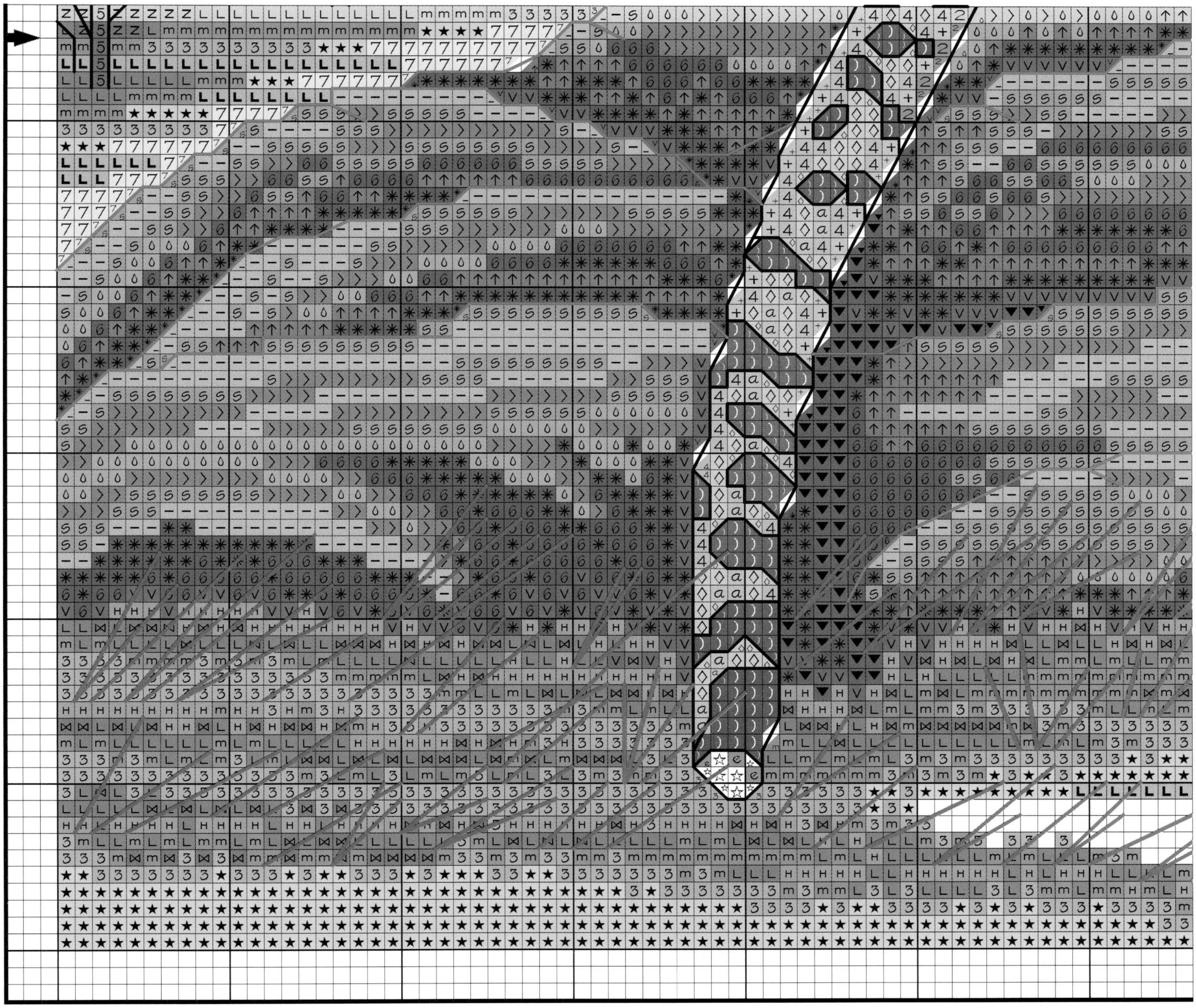

X	DMC	1/4X	B'ST	ANC.
	680		⁄ +	901
3	*680 & 725	3		901 & 305
L	*680 & 937	L		901 & 268
4	738	4		361
¢	*738 & 3782	¢		361 & 899
◊	739	◊		387
T	*739 & 3033	T		387 & 391
H	*829 & 936	H		906 & 269
	937		⁄ +	268
✱	844	✱	⁄	1041

X	DMC	1/4X	1/2X	B'ST	ANC.
V	*844 & 3371	V			1041 & 382
⋈	936				269
5	3021	5		⁄ ★	905
ʌ	3041	ʌ			871
=	*3041 & 3042	=			871 & 870 &
▼	3371	▼			382
	3743		┐		869
	3752		⁄		1032
●	310 Fr. Knot				403
	Pink area indicates last row of previous section of design.				

* Use **1** strand of each floss color listed.

† **DMC blanc** for whiskers. **DMC 436** for mouth and right side of cheetah. **DMC 501** for horizon.

★ **DMC 310** for cheetah (use **2** strands for each side of nose below eyes). **DMC 3021** for trees.

+ Use long stitches and randomly place colors when stitching grass.

Chart sections are on pgs. 38-43.
See placement diagram below.

Section 1	Section 2	Section 3
Section 4	Section 5	Section 6

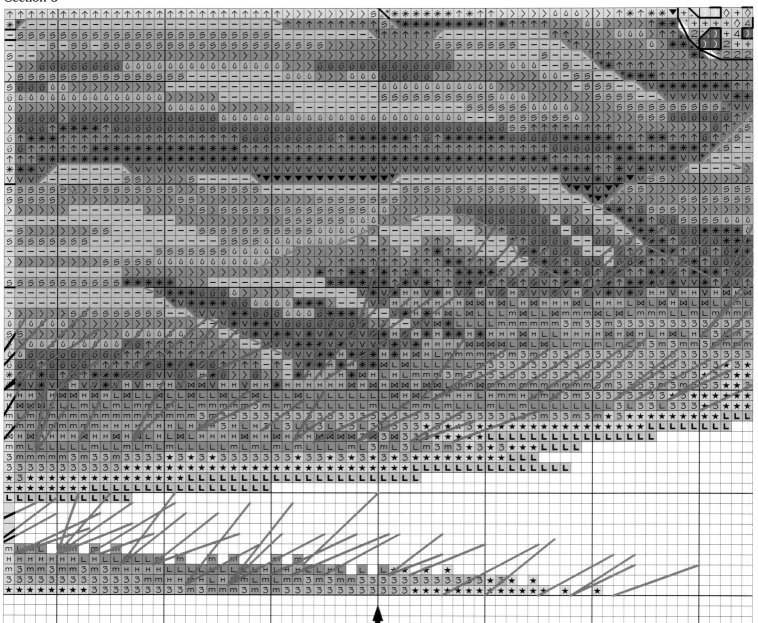

CHEETAH

X	DMC	¹/₄X	B'ST	ANC.
☆	blanc		/†	2
e	*blanc & 310	e		2 & 403
#	*blanc & 437	#		2 & 362
8	ecru	8		387
a	*ecru & 739	a		387 & 387
n	*300 & 301	n		352 & 1049
∧	*301 & 3012	∧		1049 & 844
)	310	)	/★	403

X	DMC	¹/₄X	B'ST	ANC.
◊	*372 & 647	◊		853 & 1040
⊥	435	⊥		1046
✓	*435 & 3781	✓		1046 & 904
2	436	2	/†	1045
+	*437 & 738	+		362 & 361
m	*470 & 680	m		267 & 901
$	471	$		266
♡	*471 & 502	♡		266 & 877

X	DMC	¹/₄X	B'ST	ANC.
▲	*500 & 520	▲		683 & 862
z	501	z	/†	878
✕	*502 & 522	✕		877 & 860
C	*522 & 3041	c		860 & 871
∩	*524 & 3743	∩		858 & 869
>	*613 & 648	>		831 & 900
↑	645	↑		273
6	*645 & 3012	6		273 & 844

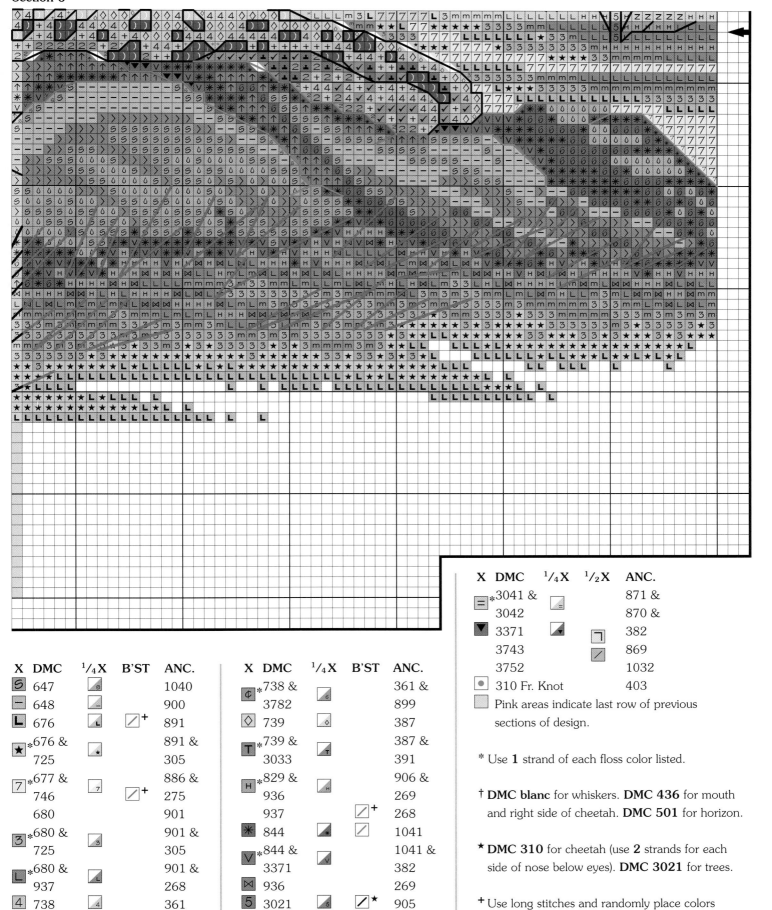

X	DMC	¹/₄X	¹/₂X	ANC.
=	*3041 &			871 &
	3042	=		870 &
▼	3371	◢	⊐	382
	3743		⟋	869
	3752			1032
⦿	310 Fr. Knot			403

▢ Pink areas indicate last row of previous sections of design.

* Use **1** strand of each floss color listed.

† **DMC blanc** for whiskers. **DMC 436** for mouth and right side of cheetah. **DMC 501** for horizon.

★ **DMC 310** for cheetah (use **2** strands for each side of nose below eyes). **DMC 3021** for trees.

⁺ Use long stitches and randomly place colors when stitching grass.

X	DMC	¹/₄X	B'ST	ANC.
S	647	s		1040
−	648	−		900
L	676	L	⟋⁺	891
★	*676 &	★		891 &
	725			305
7	*677 &	7	⟋⁺	886 &
	746			275
	680			901
3	*680 &	3		901 &
	725			305
L	*680 &	L		901 &
	937			268
4	738	4		361

X	DMC	¹/₄X	B'ST	ANC.
¢	*738 &	¢		361 &
	3782			899
◇	739	◇		387
T	*739 &	T		387 &
	3033			391
H	*829 &	H		906 &
	936			269
	937		⟋⁺	268
✳	844	✳	⟋	1041
V	*844 &	√		1041 &
	3371			382
⊠	936			269
5	3021	5	⟋★	905
▲	3041	▲		871

LION FAMILY

Section 1

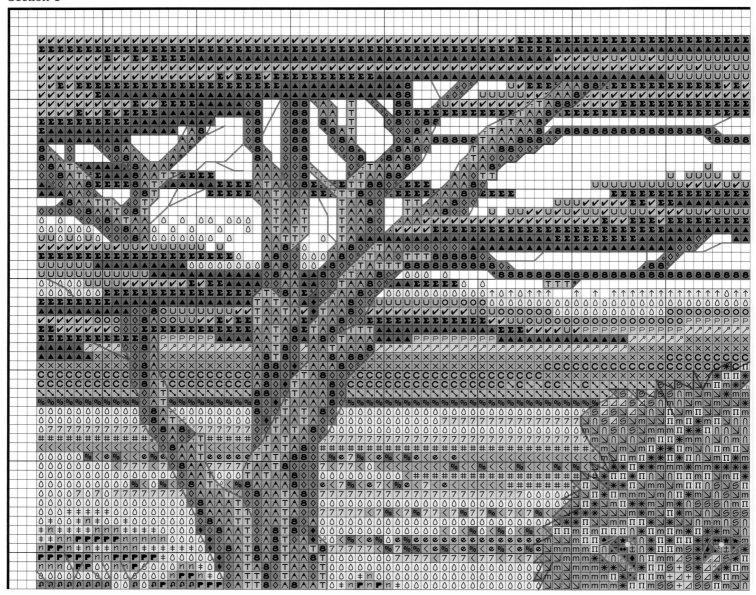

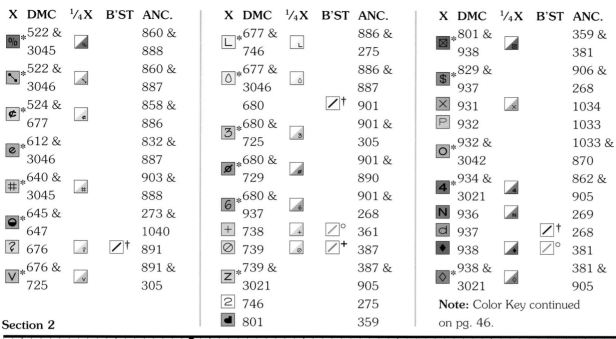

X	DMC	¼X	B'ST	ANC.
%*	522 & 3045	%		860 & 888
＼*	522 & 3046	＼		860 & 887
¢*	524 & 677	¢		858 & 886
e*	612 & 3046	e		832 & 887
#*	640 & 3045	#		903 & 888
●*	645 & 647			273 & 1040
?	676	?	╱†	891
V*	676 & 725	v		891 & 305

X	DMC	¼X	B'ST	ANC.
L*	677 & 746	L		886 & 275
◊*	677 & 3046	◊		886 & 887
	680		╱†	901
3*	680 & 725	3		901 & 305
∅*	680 & 729	∅		901 & 890
6*	680 & 937	6		901 & 268
+	738	+	╱°	361
⊘	739	⊘	╱+	387
Z*	739 & 3021			387 & 905
2	746			275
◖	801			359

X	DMC	¼X	B'ST	ANC.
⊠*	801 & 938	╱⊠		359 & 381
$*	829 & 937	$		906 & 268
✕	931	✕		1034
P	932	P		1033
O*	932 & 3042			1033 & 870
4*	934 & 3021	4		862 & 905
N	936	N		269
d	937		╱†	268
◆	938	◆	╱°	381
◊*	938 & 3021	◊		381 & 905

Note: Color Key continued on pg. 46.

Section 2

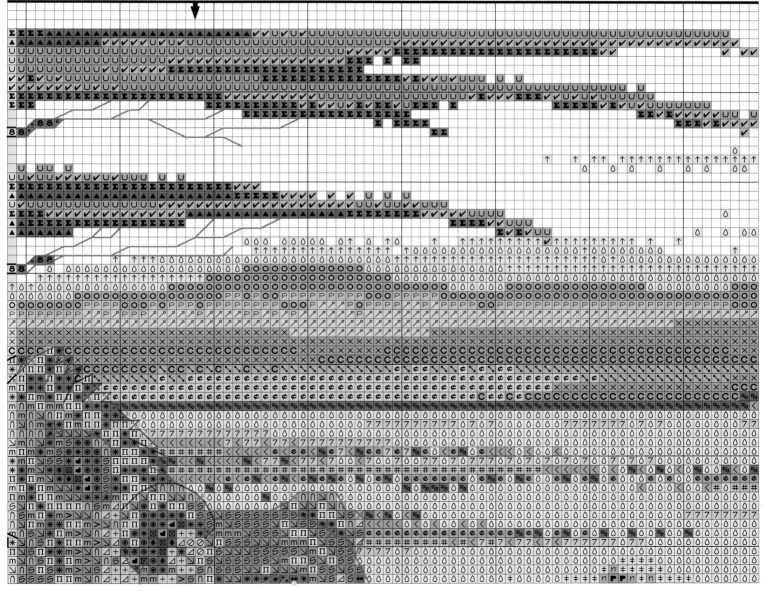

45

LION FAMILY

X	DMC	¼X	½X	B'ST	ANC.
8	3021	8		⟋△	905
T	*3022 &	T			8581 &
	3787				273
	3032			⟋★	903
<	3045	<			888
△	*3045 &				888 &
	3046				887
7	3046	7			887
	3743		↑		869

X	DMC	¼X	½X	B'ST	ANC.
◔	*3743 &				869 &
	3752				1032
	3752		◊		1032
	3781			⟋△	904
ʌ	3787	◣			273
	3790			⟋★	393
●	310 Fr. Knot				403
▨	Blue area indicates last row of previous section of design.				

* Use **1** strand of each floss color listed.

† Use long stitches and randomly place colors when stitching grass.

Note: Use long stitches for all whiskers.

★ **DMC blanc** for lioness. **DMC 3032** for right cub's chin. **DMC 3790** for left cub's chin.

+ **DMC 433** for lioness. **DMC 436** for right cub. **DMC 437** for lion's whiskers. **DMC 739** for left cub and cubs' whiskers.

○ **DMC 434** for lion and cubs. **DMC 738** for lioness's whiskers. **DMC 938** for all eyes, noses, and mouths.

△ **DMC 3021** for large tree, lioness, lion, and cubs. **DMC 3781** for small trees.

Design was stitched on a 20" x 16" piece of 28 count Antique Tan Linen (design size 13⅝" x 10") over two fabric threads. Two strands of floss were used for Cross Stitch, Half Cross Stitches, and French Knots, and 1 strand for Backstitch. It was custom framed.

Stitch Count (190w x 140h)

14 count	13⅝"	x 10"
16 count	11⅞"	x 8¾"
18 count	10⅝"	x 7⅞"

Chart sections are on pgs. 44-49. See placement diagram below.

Section 1	Section 2	Section 3
Section 4	Section 5	Section 6

Section 3

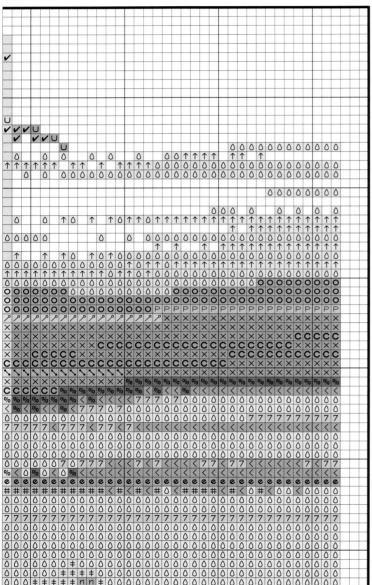

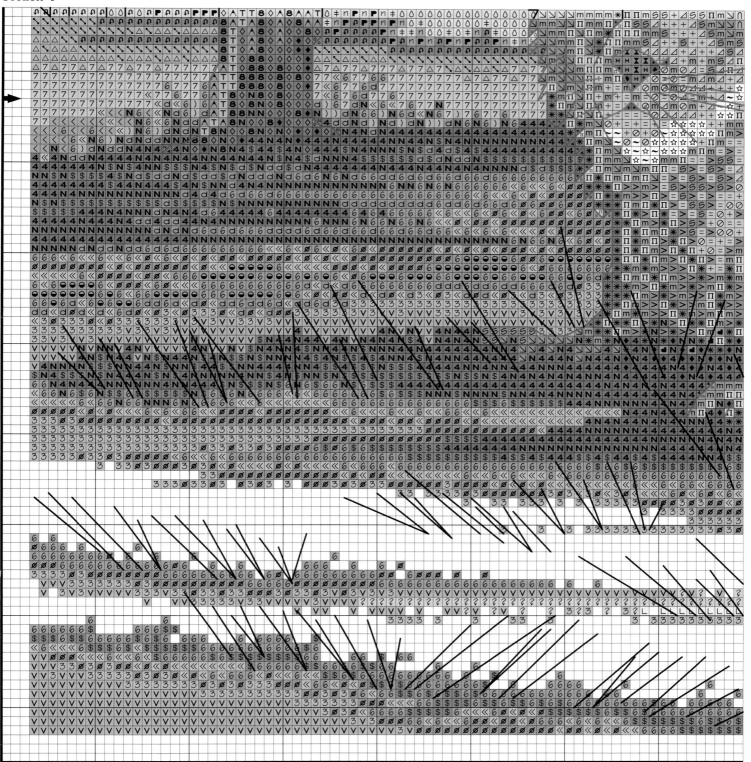

Note: Color Key located on pgs. 44-46.

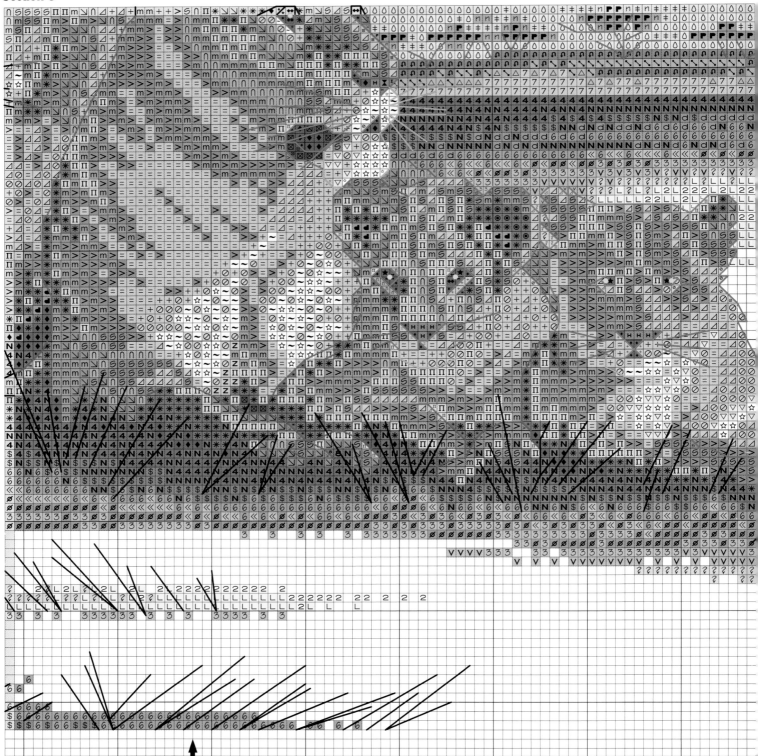

Note: Color Key located on pgs. 44-46.

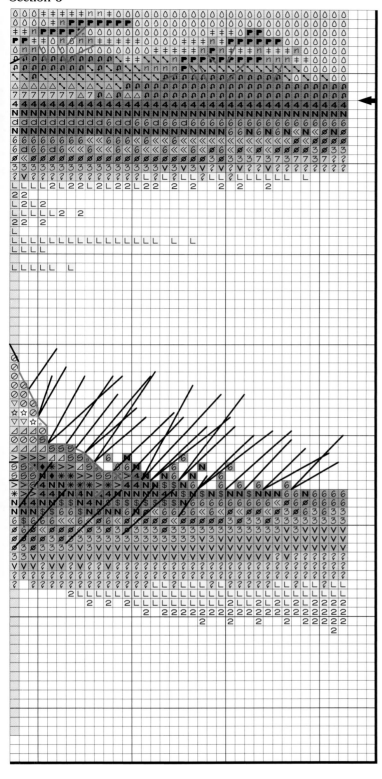

GIRAFFE

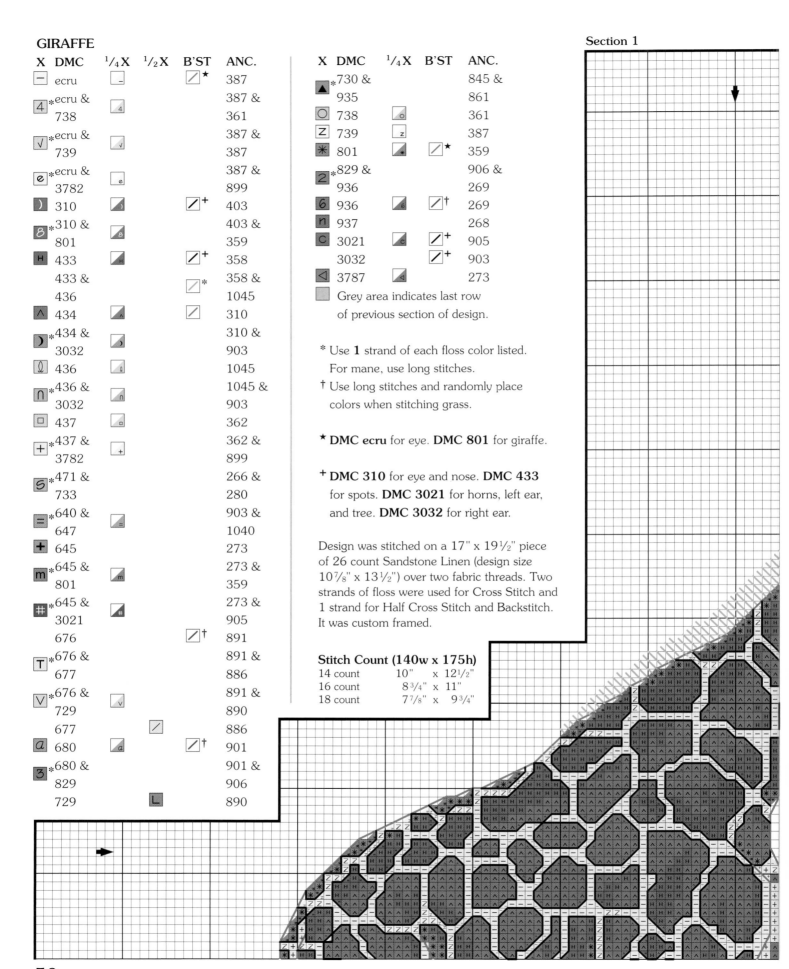

Section 1

X	DMC	1/4 X	1/2 X	B'ST	ANC.
−	ecru	−		/ ★	387
4	*ecru & 738	4			387 & 361
√	*ecru & 739	√			387 & 387
e	*ecru & 3782	e			387 & 899
)	310	)		/ +	403
8	*310 & 801	8			403 & 359
H	433	H		/ +	358
	433 & 436			/ *	358 & 1045
∧	434	∧		/	310
◗	*434 & 3032	)			310 & 903
ℓ	436	ℓ			1045
∩	436 & 3032	∩			1045 & 903
▫	437	▫			362
+	437 & 3782	+			362 & 899
S	*471 & 733				266 & 280
=	*640 & 647	=			903 & 1040
+	645				273
m	645 & 801	m			273 & 359
#	645 & 3021	#			273 & 905
	676			/ †	891
T	*676 & 677				891 & 886
V	*676 & 729	v			891 & 890
	677		/		886
a	680	a		/ †	901
3	*680 & 829				901 & 906
	729		L		890

X	DMC	1/4 X	B'ST	ANC.
▲	*730 & 935			845 & 861
O	738	o		361
Z	739	z		387
✳	801	✳	/ ★	359
2	*829 & 936			906 & 269
6	936	6	/ †	269
n	937			268
C	3021	C	/ +	905
	3032		/ +	903
◁	3787	◁		273

▢ Grey area indicates last row
  of previous section of design.

* Use **1** strand of each floss color listed.
  For mane, use long stitches.
† Use long stitches and randomly place
  colors when stitching grass.

★ **DMC ecru** for eye. **DMC 801** for giraffe.

+ **DMC 310** for eye and nose. **DMC 433**
  for spots. **DMC 3021** for horns, left ear,
  and tree. **DMC 3032** for right ear.

Design was stitched on a 17" x 19½" piece
of 26 count Sandstone Linen (design size
10⅞" x 13½") over two fabric threads. Two
strands of floss were used for Cross Stitch and
1 strand for Half Cross Stitch and Backstitch.
It was custom framed.

Stitch Count (140w x 175h)
14 count	10"	x	12½"
16 count	8¾"	x	11"
18 count	7⅞"	x	9¾"

Chart sections are on pgs. 50-53.
See placement diagram below.

Section 1	Section 2
Section 3	Section 4

GIRAFFE

X DMC	¼X	B'ST	ANC.
− ecru	−	╱ ★	387
4 * ecru & 738	4		387 & 361
√ * ecru & 739	√		387 & 387
e * ecru & 3782	e		387 & 899
) 310	)	╱ +	403
8 * 310 & 801	8		403 & 359
H 433	H	╱ +	358

X DMC	¼X	B'ST	ANC.
433 & 436		╱ *	358 & 1045
∧ 434	◢	╱	310
) * 434 & 3032	)		310 & 903
◖ 436	◣		1045
∩ * 436 & 3032	∩		1045 & 903
▢ 437	▢		362
+ * 437 & 3782	+		362 & 899

X DMC	¼X	B'ST	ANC.
S * 471 & 733			266 & 280
= * 640 & 647	=		903 & 1040
+ 645			273
m * 645 & 801	m		273 & 359
# 645 & 3021	#		273 & 905
676		╱ †	891
T * 676 & 677			891 & 886

X	DMC	¼X	½X	B'ST	ANC.
V	*676 &	v			891 &
	729				890
	677		/		886
a	680	a		/†	901
3	*680 &				901 &
	829				906
	729		L		890
▲	*730 &				845 &
	935				861
O	738	o			361
Z	739	z			387
✳	801	*		/★	359

X	DMC	¼X	B'ST	ANC.
2	*829 &			906 &
	936			269
6	936	6	/†	269
n	937			268
C	3021	c	/+	905
	3032		/+	903
◁	3787			273
	Grey areas indicate last row of previous sections of design.			

* Use **1** strand of each floss color listed.
For mane, use long stitches.

† Use long stitches and randomly place colors when stitching grass.

★ **DMC ecru** for eye. **DMC 801** for giraffe.

+ **DMC 310** for eye and nose.
DMC 433 for spots. **DMC 3021** for horns, left ear, and tree.
DMC 3032 for right ear.

53

ELEPHANT

X DMC	¼X	ANC.	X DMC	¼X	ANC.	X DMC	¼X	B'ST	ANC.	X DMC	¼X	B'ST	ANC.
☆ blanc	⬚	2	L *453 & 842	L	231 & 1080	X *503 & 523	x		876 & 859	V *680 & 729	√		901 & 890
△ *blanc & 453	△	2 & 231	Z *471 & 502	z	266 & 877	O *503 & 3041	o		876 & 871	6 *680 & 733	6		901 & 280
⊥ *451 & 839	◢	233 & 1086	n *471 & 524	n	266 & 858	√ *524 & 3042	√		858 & 870	729			730
4 *452 & 840	4	232 & 1084	▲ *500 & 520	▲	683 & 862	7 676	7		891	730		╱†	890
+ 453	+	231	S *501 & 522	s	878 & 860	◇ *676 & 729	◇		891 & 890	H *730 & 829	H	╱†	845
C *453 & 841	c	231 & 1082				✓ 677	✓	╱†	886	m *838 & 3021	m		845 & 906
						3 680	3		901	T 3021	T	╱	1088 & 905
													905

Section 1

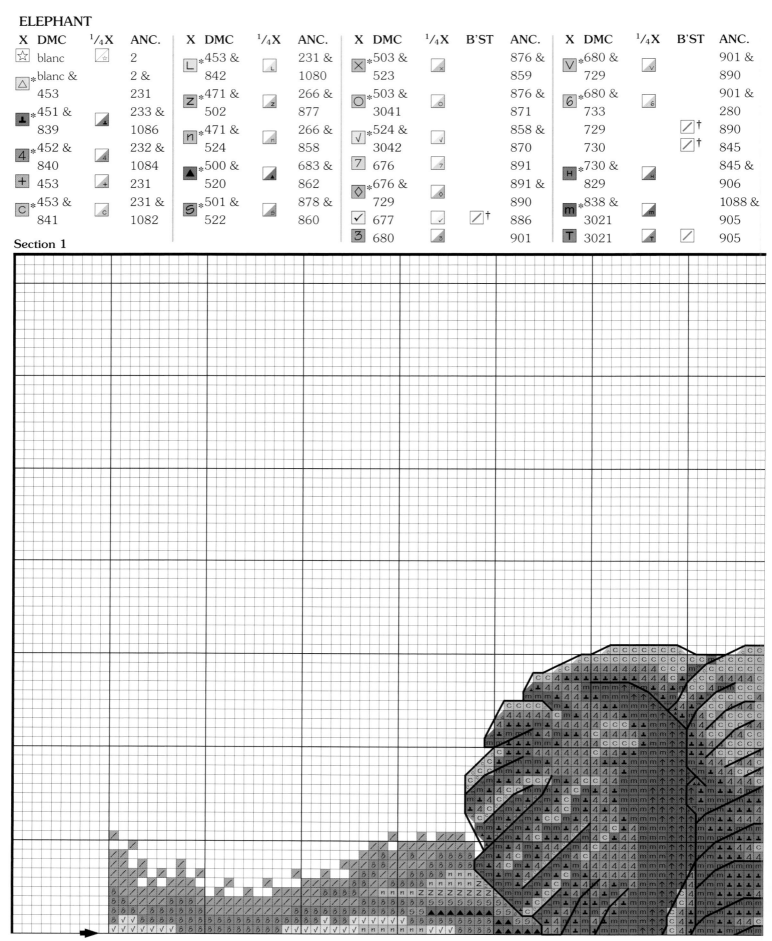

X	DMC	¼X	½X	B'ST	ANC.
	3042		8		870
	3042 &		⟋ *		870 &
	3752				1032
↑	3371	↗		⟋	382
e	3781	e			904

Grey area indicates last row of previous section of design.

Design was stitched on a 16" x 16" piece of 28 count Shell Linen (design size 10" x 10") over two fabric threads. Two strands of floss were used for Cross Stitch and Half Cross Stitch and 1 strand for Backstitch. It was custom framed.

Stitch Count (140w x 140h)

14 count	10"	x	10"
16 count	8¾"	x	8¾"
18 count	7⅞"	x	7⅞"

* Use **1** strand of each floss color listed.
† Use long stitches and randomly place colors when stitching grass.

Section 2

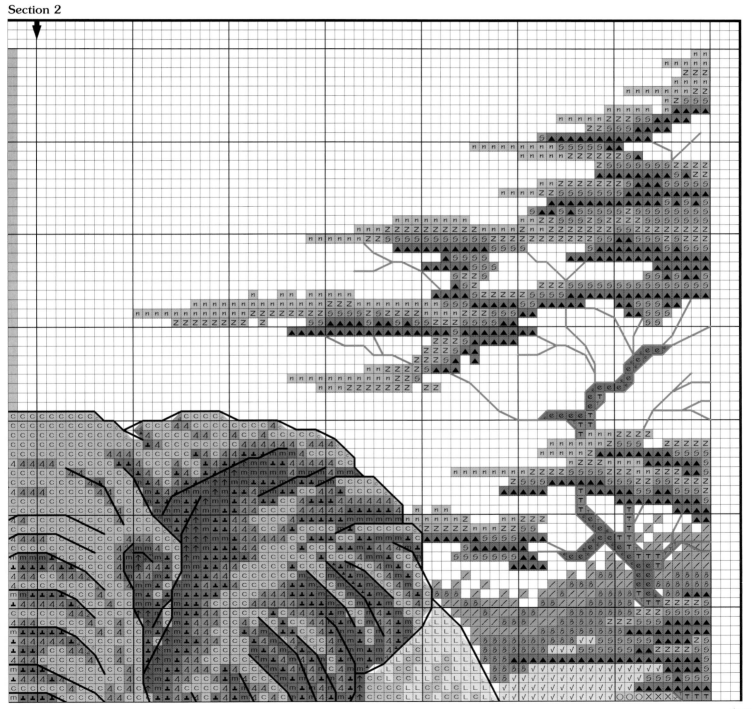

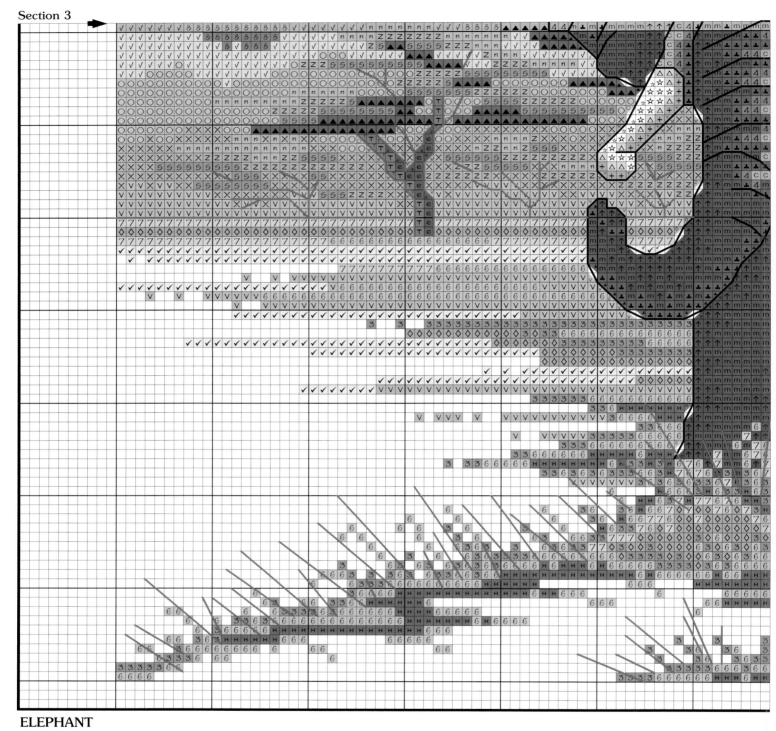

ELEPHANT

X	DMC	¹/₄X	ANC.	X	DMC	¹/₄X	ANC.	X	DMC	¹/₄X	B'ST	ANC.	X	DMC	¹/₄X	B'ST	ANC.
☆	blanc		2	L	*453 & 842	L	231 & 1080	X	*503 & 523	×		876 & 859	V	*680 & 729	√		901 & 890
△	*blanc & 453		2 & 231	Z	*471 & 502	z	266 & 877	O	*503 & 3041	o		876 & 871	6	*680 & 733	6		901 & 280
⊥	*451 & 839	⊿	233 & 1086	n	*471 & 524	n	266 & 858	√	*524 & 3042	√		858 & 870		729 730		/† /†	890 845
4	*452 & 840	4	232 & 1084	▲	*500 & 520	▲	683 & 862	7	676	7		891	H	*730 & 829	н		845 & 906
+	453	+	231	S	*501 & 522	s	878 & 860	◇	*676 & 729	◇		891 & 890	m	*838 & 3021	m		1088 & 905
C	*453 & 841	c	231 & 1082					✔	677	✔	/†	886	T	3021	T	/	905
								3	680	3		901					

Section 4

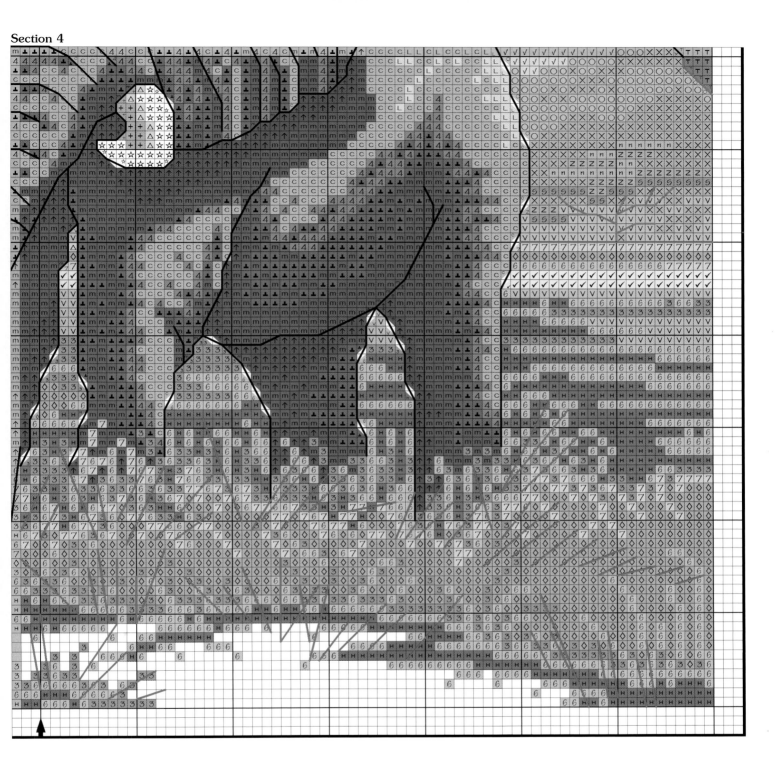

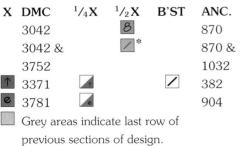

X	DMC	¼X	½X	B'ST	ANC.
	3042		8		870
	3042 &		╱*		870 &
	3752				1032
↑	3371	↑		╱	382
e	3781	e			904

☐ Grey areas indicate last row of
previous sections of design.

Chart sections are on pgs. 54-57.
See placement diagram below.

Section 1	Section 2
Section 3	Section 4

* Use **1** strand of each floss color listed.

† Use long stitches and randomly place colors when stitching grass.

ZEBRA

X	DMC	¼X	B'ST	ANC.
☆	blanc	☆	╱★	2
8	310	8	╱	403
●	*310 & 898	●	◢	403 & 360
4	413	4		236
+	414	+	╱★	235
S	415	S		398
∧	*415 & 3782	∧		398 & 899
e	*415 & 3799			398 & 236
↘	*434 & 898	↘		310 & 360
−	471	−		266

X	DMC	¼X	B'ST	ANC.
I	*471 & 502			266 & 877
▲	*500 & 520	▲		683 & 862
Z	501 502	Z	╱★	878 877
X	*502 & 522	X		877 & 860
C	*522 & 3041	C		860 & 871
a	676	a	╱†	891
V	*676 & 725	V		891 & 305
✓	677	✓		886

X	DMC	¼X	B'ST	ANC.
O	*677 & 746	o		886 & 275
3	*680 & 725	3		
6	*680 & 829 746	6	╱†	901 & 906 275
n	762	n		234
=	*762 & 3033	=		234 & 391
⊥	*829 & 936 898 937	⊥	╱+ ╱†	906 & 269 360 268

Section 1

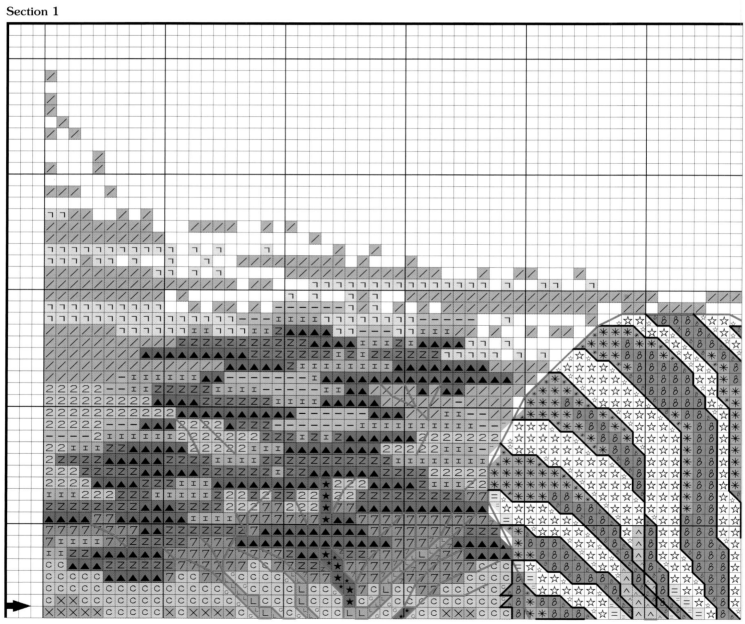

X DMC	¼X	½X	B'ST	ANC.
3031			⧄ +	905
L 3032	⌐			903
7 3041	7			871
2 *3041 &				871 &
3042				870
3743		⌐		869
3752		⧄		1032
★ 3781	★			904
✳ 3799	✳		⧄	236

Pink area indicates last row of previous section of design.

★ **DMC blanc** for eyes. **DMC 414** for ears.
DMC 502 for horizon.

+ **DMC 898** for mane. **DMC 3031** for trees.

Design was stitched on an 18½" x 13½" piece of 26 count White Birch Heatherfield (design size 12⅜" x 7¼") over two fabric threads. Two strands of floss were used for Cross Stitch and 1 strand for Backstitch. It was custom framed.

Stitch Count (160w x 94h)

14 count	11½"	x 6¾"
16 count	10"	x 5⅞"
18 count	9"	x 5¼"

* Use **1** strand of each floss color listed.
† Use long stitches and randomly place colors when stitching grass.

Chart sections are on pgs. 58-63. See placement diagram below.

Section 1	Section 2	Section 3
Section 4	Section 5	Section 6

Section 2

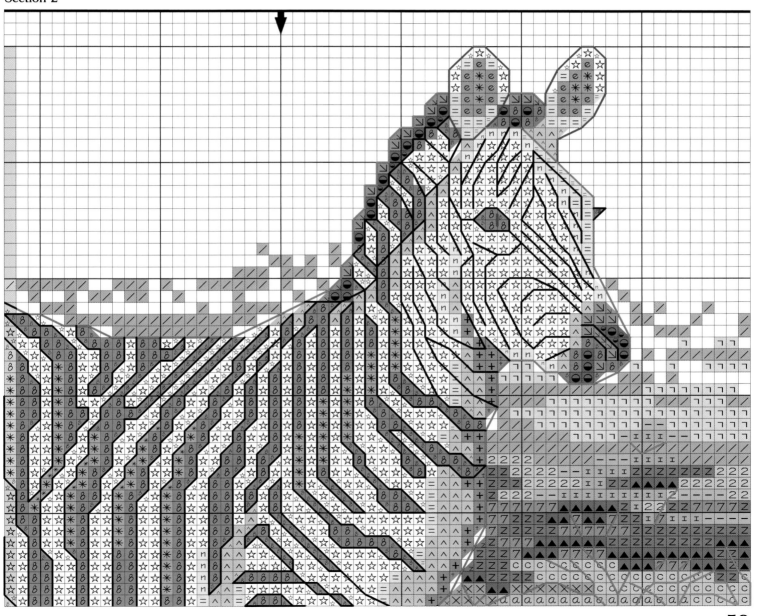

59

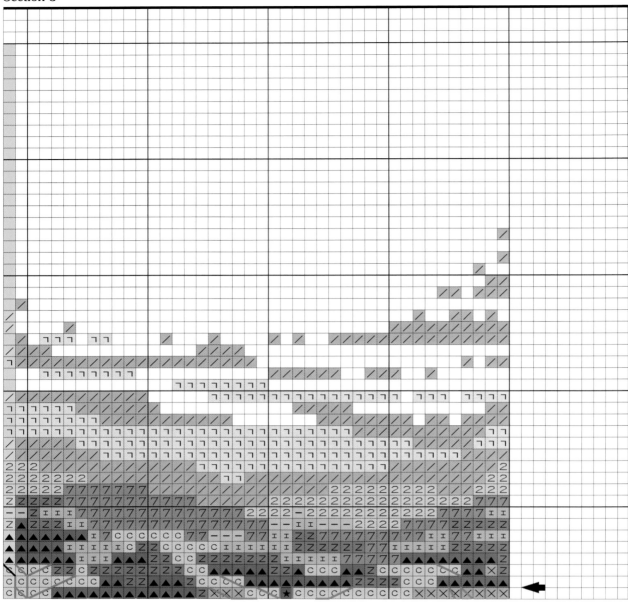

ZEBRA

X	DMC	¼X	B'ST	ANC.
☆	blanc	⊿	╱★	2
8	310		╱	403
●	*310 & 898	●		403 & 360
4	413	4		236
+	414	+	╱★	235
5	415	5		398
∧	*415 & 3782	∧		398 & 899
e	*415 & 3799	e		398 & 236
⅃	*434 & 898	⅃		310 & 360
−	471	−		266

X	DMC	¼X	B'ST	ANC.
I	*471 & 502			266 & 877
▲	*500 & 520	▲		683 & 862
Z	501 502	z	╱★	878 877
X	*502 & 522	x		877 & 860
C	*522 & 3041	c		860 & 871
a	676	a	╱†	891
V	*676 & 725	V		891 & 305
✓	677	✓		886

X	DMC	¼X	B'ST	ANC.
O	*677 & 746	o		886 & 275
3	*680 & 725	3		901 & 906
6	*680 & 829 746	6	╱†	275
n	762	n		234
=	*762 & 3033	=		234 & 391
⊥	*829 & 936	⊿		906 & 269
	898		╱+	360
	937		╱†	268

60

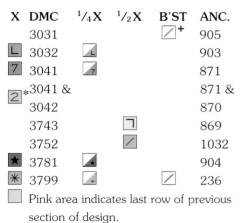

X	DMC	¼X	½X	B'ST	ANC.
	3031			⌐+	905
L	3032	L			903
7	3041	7			871
2 *	3041 &				871 &
	3042				870
	3743		⌐		869
	3752		⌐		1032
★	3781	◢			904
✳	3799	◢		⌐	236

★ DMC blanc for eyes. DMC 414 for ears.
DMC 502 for horizon.

+ DMC 898 for mane. DMC 3031 for trees.

Pink area indicates last row of previous
section of design.

* Use **1** strand of each floss color listed.
† Use long stitches and randomly place colors when stitching grass.

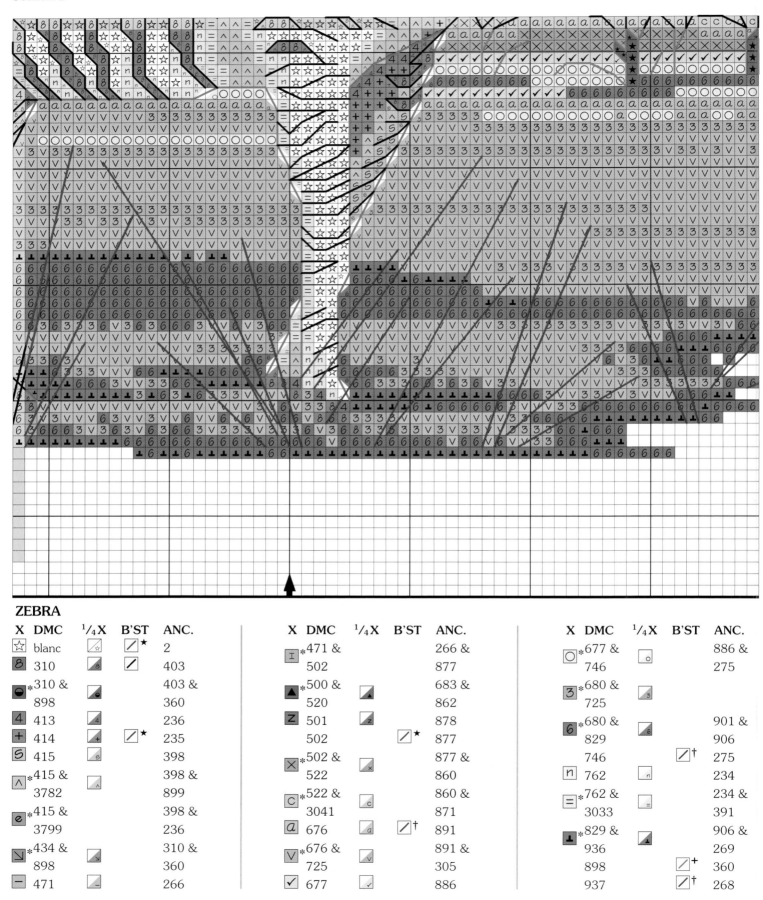

ZEBRA

X	DMC	¼X	B'ST	ANC.
☆	blanc	⊘	╱★	2
8	310	8	╱	403
●	*310 & 898	●		403 & 360
4	413	4		236
+	414	+	╱★	235
S	415	s		398
∧	*415 & 3782	∧		398 & 899
e	*415 & 3799	e		398 & 236
∨	*434 & 898	∨		310 & 360
−	471	−		266

X	DMC	¼X	B'ST	ANC.
I	*471 & 502			266 & 877
▲	*500 & 520	▲		683 & 862
Z	501 502	z	╱★	878 877
X	*502 & 522	x		877 & 860
C	*522 & 3041	c		860 & 871
a	676	a	╱†	891
∨	*676 & 725	∨		891 & 305
✓	677	✓		886

X	DMC	¼X	B'ST	ANC.
○	*677 & 746	o		886 & 275
3	*680 & 725	3		
6	*680 & 829 746	6	╱†	901 & 906 275
n	762	n		234
=	*762 & 3033	=		234 & 391
⊥	*829 & 936 898 937	⊥	╱+ ╱†	906 & 269 360 268

Section 6

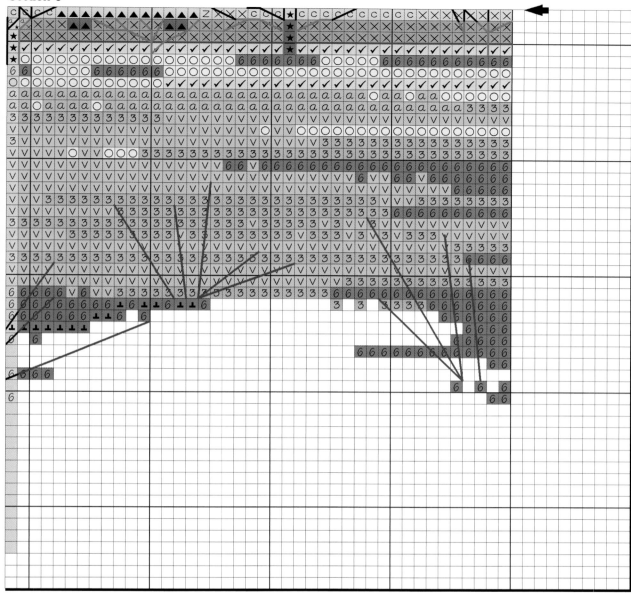

X	DMC	¼X	½X	B'ST	ANC.
	3031			◿+	905
L	3032	◣			903
7	3041	◢			871
2	*3041 &				871 &
	3042				870
	3743		◥		869
	3752		◿		1032
★	3781	◢			904
✳	3799	◢		◿	236

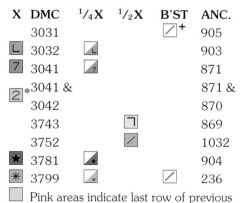 Pink areas indicate last row of previous sections of design.

★ **DMC blanc** for eyes. **DMC 414** for ears.
DMC 502 for horizon.

+ **DMC 898** for mane. **DMC 3031** for trees.

* Use **1** strand of each floss color listed.

† Use long stitches and randomly place colors when stitching grass.

CALADIUMS

X	DMC	ANC.
☆	*blanc	2
◗	†310	403
▲	*319	218
V	*347	1025
m	367	217
=	368	214
2	369	1043
3	*498	1005
✕	*500	683
6	*501	878

X	DMC	ANC.
△	*502	877
C	503	876
7	504	1042
L	*760	1022
8	*761	1021
+	*815	43
✳	*902	897
O	*3328	1024

☐ Grey area indicates last row
  of previous section of design.

* You will need **3** skeins of floss.
† You will need **4** skeins of floss.
★ You will need **2** skeins of floss.

Design was stitched on a 20" x 20" piece of 20 count
Ivory Jobelan (design size 14" x 14") over two fabric
threads. Four strands of floss were used for Cross Stitch.
It was custom framed.

Stitch Count (140w x 140h)

14 count	10"	x 10"
16 count	8³⁄₄"	x 8³⁄₄"
18 count	7⁷⁄₈"	x 7⁷⁄₈"

Section 1

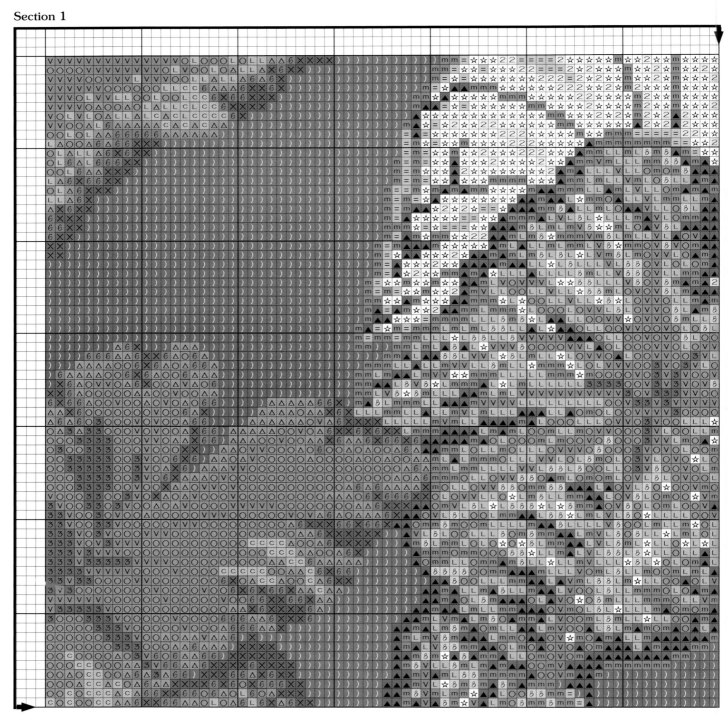

Chart sections are on pgs. 64-67.
See placement diagram below.

Section 1	Section 2
Section 3	Section 4

Section 2

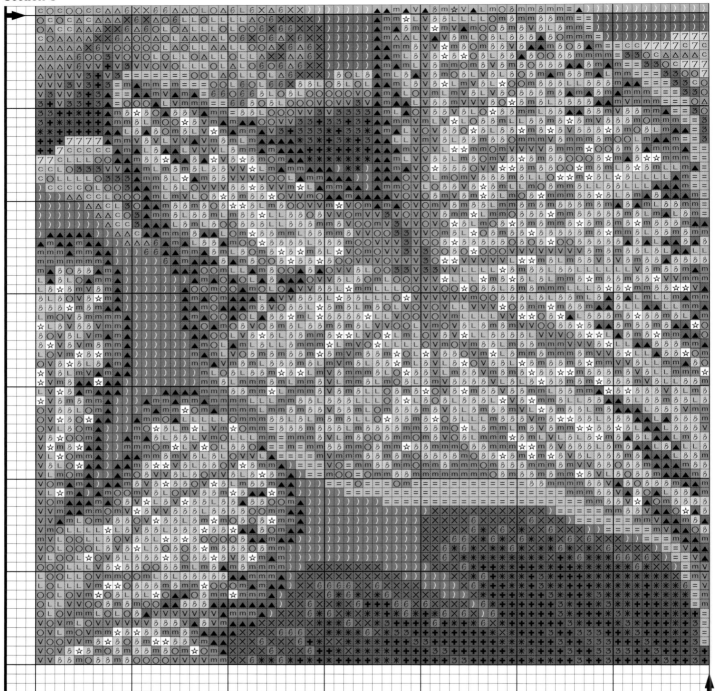

CALADIUMS

X	DMC	ANC.
☆*	blanc	2
)†	310	403
▲*	319	218
V*	347	1025
m*	367	217
=	368	214
2	369	1043
3*	498	1005
X*	500	683
6*	501	878

X	DMC	ANC.
△*	502	877
C	503	876
7	504	1042
L*	760	1022
8*	761	1021
+*	815	43
*＊	902	897
O*	3328	1024
▨	Grey areas indicate last row of previous sections of design.	

* You will need **3** skeins of floss.
† You will need **4** skeins of floss.
★ You will need **2** skeins of floss.

WATER LILIES

X	DMC	ANC.
☆*blanc	2
4*221	897
ⓐ 223	895
L†310	403
✱†311	148
⊥ 319	218
△*320	215
8 335	38
6*367	217
○*368	214

X	DMC	ANC.
─ 369	1043
◔ 414	235
℮ 415	398
Z 434	310
✓ 725	305
5 727	293
◓ 783	306
★ 801	359
= 818	23
◇*823	152

X	DMC	ANC.
2 831	277
∩ 834	874
¢ 890	218
✕ 934	862
m 936	269
◣ 938	381
+ 975	355
∽ 976	1001
‹ 977	1002
3 3011	846

X	DMC	ANC.
❭†3012	844
I*3013	842
V 3326	36
7 3721	896
C 3722	1027

Grey area indicates last row of previous section of design.

* You will need **2** skeins of floss.
† You will need **3** skeins of floss.
★ You will need **5** skeins of floss.

Section 1

68

Design was stitched on a 20" x 20" piece of 20 count Ivory Jobelan (design size 14" x 14") over two fabric threads. Four strands of floss were used for Cross Stitch. It was custom framed.

Stitch Count (140w x 140h)

14 count	10"	x	10"
16 count	8³/₄"	x	8³/₄"
18 count	7⁷/₈"	x	7⁷/₈"

Chart sections are on pgs. 68-71.
See placement diagram below.

Section 1	Section 2
Section 3	Section 4

Section 2

WATER LILIES

X	DMC	ANC.
☆*	blanc	2
4*	221	897
a	223	895
L†	310	403
*†	311	148
⊥	319	218
△★	320	215
8	335	38
6*	367	217
○*	368	214

X	DMC	ANC.
−	369	1043
◌	414	235
e	415	398
Z	434	310
✓	725	305
5	727	293
◑	783	306
★	801	359
=	818	23
◇*	823	152

X	DMC	ANC.
2	831	277
∩	834	874
¢	890	218
✕	934	862
m	936	269
◣	938	381
+	975	355
~	976	1001
‹	977	1002
3	3011	846

X	DMC	ANC.
> †	3012	844
I *	3013	842
V	3326	36
7	3721	896
C	3722	1027
▢	Grey areas indicate last row of previous sections of design.	

* You will need **2** skeins of floss.

† You will need **3** skeins of floss.

★ You will need **5** skeins of floss.

X	DMC	¼X	B'ST	ANC.
☆	blanc			2
H	*blanc & 415			2 & 398
<	*blanc & 469			2 & 267
L	*blanc & 722			2 & 323
◇	300			352
8	*300 & 310			352 & 403
⋒	301			1049
⊼	*301 & 402			1049 & 1047
I	310	◢	╱†	403
6	312	◢		979
✓	318			399
2	322	◢		978
V	334		╱†	977
e	336	◢	╱	150
♠	349			13
4	355		╱†	1014
◗	*367 & 502			217 & 877
⊥	*368 & 3325			214 & 129
	402		╱†	1047
	414		╱†	235
3	415			398
z	433		╱★	358
✕	469		╱†	267
7	470			267
△	*470 & 741			267 & 304
5	471	◢5	╱†	266
y	*471 & 743			266 & 302
¢	*471 & 776			266 & 24
╱	472			253
★	501		╱★	878
⊠	*501 & 502			878 & 877
✳	632			936
T	645	◢	╱†	273
m	*645 & 3021	◢m		273 & 905
∿	720			326
√	721			925
∧	722			323

X	DMC	B'ST	ANC.
$	729	╱†	890
✕	733		280
+	741	╱†	304
>	742		303
=	743		302
(	744	╱★	301
↘	776		24
9	833		907
~	898		360
a	899		52
c	920	╱	1004
⋒	936	╱†	269
◆	*936 & 3021		269 & 905
◣	3021	╱	905
S	3022		8581
↑	3023		1040
⊥	3031		905
—	3325		129
●	blanc Fr. Knot		2
●	310 Fr. Knot		403

▦ Grey area indicates last row
of previous section of design.

* Use **1** strand of each floss color listed.

† DMC **310** for bluebird's eye and tire swing.
DMC **334** for clouds. DMC **355** for silo.
DMC **402** for chipmunk's whiskers (use
long stitches). DMC **414** for dogwoods.
DMC **469** for trees and ground. DMC **471**
for inner border. DMC **645** for bluebird's beak.
DMC **729** for robins' beaks. DMC **741**
for daffodil. DMC **936** for stems and grass
(use long stitches).

★ DMC **433** for dogwoods (**2** strands), fence,
and rope. DMC **501** for ground. DMC **744**
for daffodil (use long stitches).

Design was stitched on a 14" x 14" piece of
14 count Fiddler's Lite Aida (design size 7 7/8" x 7 7/8").
Two strands of floss were used for Cross Stitch and
French Knots and 1 strand for Backstitch except
where noted in key. It was custom framed.

Stitch Count (110w x 110h)

14 count	7 7/8"	x	7 7/8"
16 count	6 7/8"	x	6 7/8"
18 count	6 1/8"	x	6 1/8"

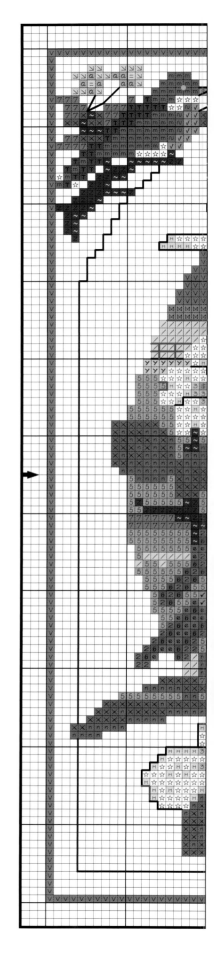

SUMMER GARDEN

X	DMC	B'ST	ANC.
☆	blanc		2
T	*blanc & 415		2 & 398
◢	300	◩†	352
)	310		403
▲	*310 & 355		403 & 1014
⊘	318		399
△	347		1025
⊥	349		13
7	355		1014
4	400		351
2	415		398
6	469	◩★	267
m	*469 & 471		267 & 266
↑	470		267
L	471		266
▶	*471 & 725		266 & 305
✓	472		253
+	502	◩	877
◁	503		876
	606	◩†	334
C	*606 & 740		334 & 316
8	*606 & 817		334 & 13
I	611	◩★	898
∩	612		832
a	613		831
◿	644	◩	830
Z	*644 & 3053		830 & 261
e	676		891
n	720	◩★	326
+	721		925
V	722		323
★	725		305
=	740		316
S	*740 & 741		316 & 304
◕	741		304
♡	760		1022
	817	◩★	13
▷	822		390
H	842	◩★	1080
~	920		1004
◇	921		1003

X	DMC	B'ST	ANC.
◀	922		1003
✕	934		862
▲	936		269
◐	938	◩★	381
✳	3051		681
3	3052		262
⟩	3053		261
−	3325	◩★	129
$	3328		1024
⦿	blanc		2
▨	Grey area indicates last row of previous section of design.		

* Use **1** strand of each floss color listed.

† **DMC 300** for field and road.
   DMC 606 for tomatoes.

★ **DMC 469** for carrot tops, tomato stems, trees and ground under trees. **DMC 611** for whiskers (use long stitches). **DMC 720** for carrots. **DMC 817** for inner border. **DMC 842** for radish. **DMC 938** for ground. **DMC 3325** for clouds.

Design was stitched on a 14" x 14" piece of 14 count Fiddler's Lite (design size 7 7/8" x 7 7/8"). Two strands of floss were used for Cross Stitch and French Knots and 1 strand for Backstitch. It was custom framed.

Stitch Count (110w x 110h)
14 count	7 7/8"	x 7 7/8"
16 count	6 7/8"	x 6 7/8"
18 count	6 1/8"	x 6 1/8"

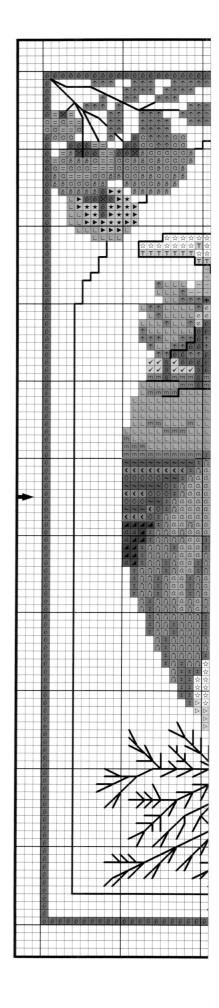

FALL HARVESTTIME

X	DMC	¼X	B'ST	ANC.
☆	blanc			2
(	*blanc & 648	◖		2 & 900
#	*blanc & 928			2 & 274
P	*blanc & 3041			2 & 871
Z	300			352
⊥	*300 & 400			352 & 351
✔	*300 & 3031			352 & 905
∧	301		╱†	1049
C	*301 & 922			1049 & 1003
)	*310	◢		403
¢	355			1014
♠	400		╱†	351
◆	*400 & 470			351 & 267
♥	*400 & 3031			351 & 905
X	*420 & 646			374 & 8581
L	*420 & 647			374 & 1040
◇	469			267
S	*469 & 815			267 & 43
8	501		╱★	878
4	*501 & 921			878 & 1003
U	*502 & 922			877 & 1003
$	610		╱★	889
e	611			898
↑	645		╱★	273
5	*645 & 3021			273 & 905
V	646			8581
m	647			1040
★	720		╱†	326
R	*720 & 971			326 & 316
<	721			925
=	725			305
>	*725 & 783			305 & 306
3	730		╱	845

X	DMC	B'ST	ANC.
+	733	╱★	280
7	734		279
T	740		316
↘	*783 & 922		306 & 1003
H	815	╱†	43
⊠	833		907
¢	834		874
	844	╱	1041
2	920		1004
◊	921		1003
∞	922		1003
★	926		850
N	927	╱★	848
O	928		274
▲	936	╱★	269
C	972		298
✳	3012	╱	844
∧	3013		842
6	3021	╱†	905
7	3023		1040
●	3031	╱	905
▼	3041		871
●	blanc Fr. Knot		2
☐	Pink area indicates last row of previous section of design.		

* Use **1** strand of each floss color listed.

† **DMC 301** for inner border. **DMC 400** for large pumpkin. **DMC 720** for small pumpkins. **DMC 815** for tree. **DMC 3021** for acorns.

★ **DMC 501** for horizon. **DMC 610** for ground. **DMC 645** for whiskers (use long stitches). **DMC 733** for grass (use long stitches). **DMC 927** for clouds. **DMC 936** for ground below porch and road.

Design was stitched on a 14" x 14" piece of 14 count Fiddler's Lite Aida (design size 7⅞" x 7⅞"). Two strands of floss were used for Cross Stitch and French Knots and 1 strand for Backstitch. It was custom framed.

Stitch Count (110w x 110h)

14 count	7⅞" x	7⅞"
16 count	6⅞" x	6⅞"
18 count	6⅛" x	6⅛"

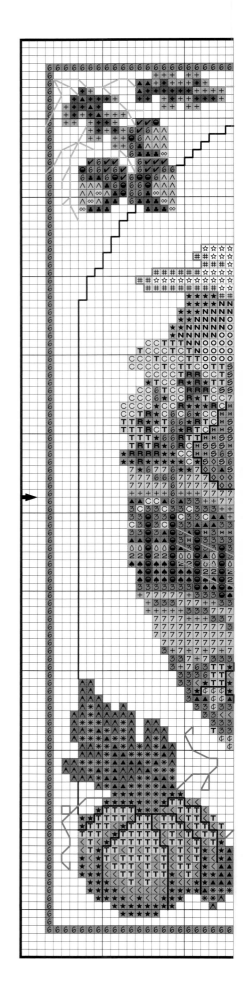

X	DMC	¼X	B'ST	ANC.
☆	blanc	☆		2
X	*blanc & 367			2 & 217
−	*blanc & 415			2 & 398
~	*blanc & 503			2 & 876
T	*blanc & 648			2 & 900
◿	*blanc & 932	◿		2 & 1033
L	*blanc & 3041			2 & 871
◥	304	◥	╱★	1006
)	310	)	╱+	403
H	*310 & 413			403 & 236
Z	311			148
n	319		╱★	218
5	320			215
♡	321	♡	╱★	9046
◁	*334 & 932			977 & 1033
6	367		╱+	217
◇	*402 & 842			1047 & 1080
◢	413			236
e	414		╱†	235
+	415			398
9	433	9	╱	358
=	434		╱+	310
7	*435 & 611			1046 & 898
	500		╱★	683
↑	*500 & 501			683 & 878
O	*501 & 502			878 & 877
✓	611		╱★	898
L	613			831
5	645	◿	╱	273
m	*645 & 3032			273 & 903
⊥	646			8581
◼	*646 & 3021			8581 & 905
∩	647			1040
⊗	648		╱	900

X	DMC	¼X	B'ST	ANC.
>	*648 & 738			900 & 361
∪	*648 & 739			900 & 387
C	738			361
✳	801	◿		359
8	815			43
⊥	838			1088
a	841	a		1082
<	842			1080
4	844	4		1041
△	890	◿	╱+	218
3	930		╱★	1035
X	931			1034
V	932	◿		1033
Y	938			381
∧	963			73
0	3021		╱+	905
2	3032			903
I	3041			871
●	310 Fr. Knot			403

▢ Grey area indicates last row of previous section of design.

* Use **1** strand of each floss color listed.

† Use long stitches for whiskers.

★ **DMC 304** for inner border. **DMC 319** for trees. **DMC 321** for cardinals. **DMC 500** for ground. **DMC 611** for chimney. **DMC 930** for all other.

+ **DMC 310** for cardinals. **DMC 434** for twigs. **DMC 890** for trees and pine needles. (**Note:** For pine needles, stitch 890 first and then stitch 367 over 890 and use long stitches.) **DMC 3021** for cabin.

Design was stitched on a 14" x 14" piece of 14 count Fiddler's Lite Aida (design size 7⅞" x 7⅞"). Two strands of floss were used for Cross Stitch and French Knots and 1 strand for Backstitch. It was custom framed.

Stitch Count (110w x 110h)

14 count	7⅞"	x 7⅞"
16 count	6⅞"	x 6⅞"
18 count	6⅛"	x 6⅛"

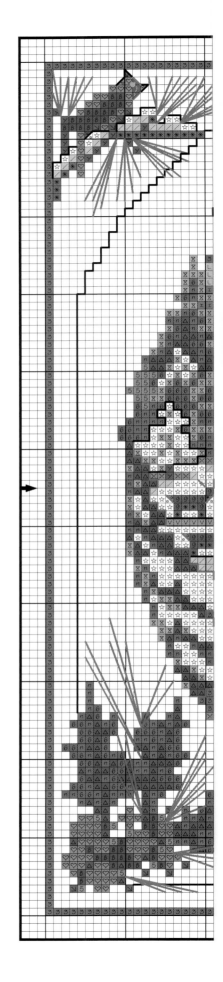

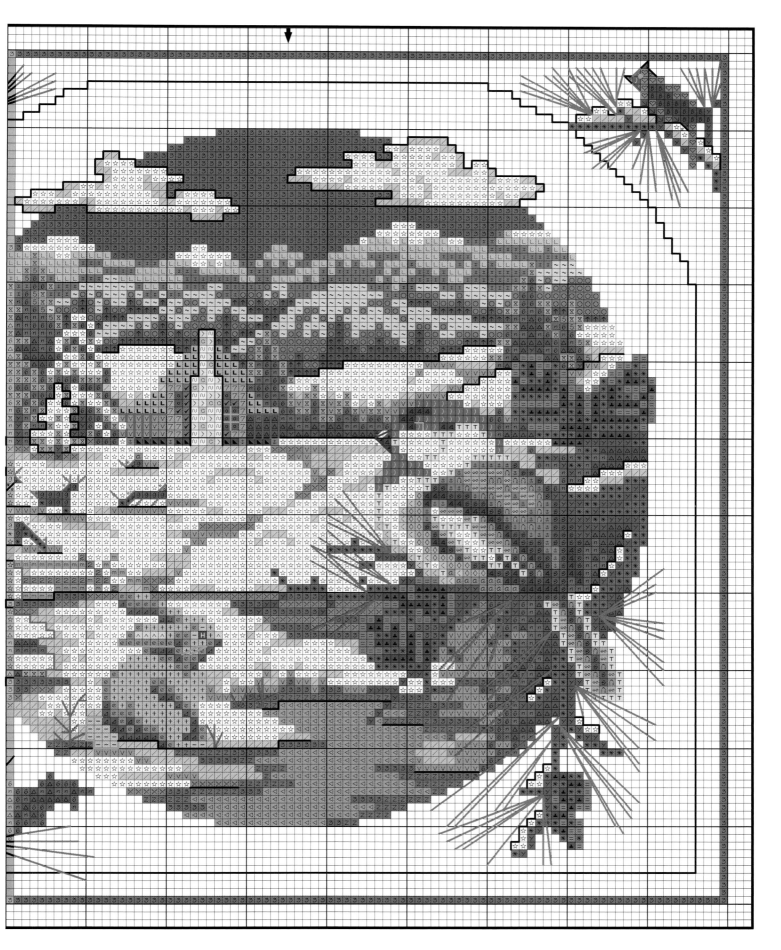

FLORA SAMPLER

X	DMC	B'ST	ANC.
Σ	*520	╱★	862
=	676		891
╱	677		886
X	†729		890
♡	†760		1022
■	839		1086
✳	840		1084
V	927		848
6	†3052	╱	262
3	3328		1024
m	†3768		779

	DMC	STITCH
✳	°	Eyelet Stitch, pg. 96
	3052	Satin Stitch, pg. 96
	3328	Plait Stitch, pg. 96
	3768	Rice Stitch, pg. 96
		Grey area indicates last row of previous section of design.

* You will need **3** skeins of floss.

† You will need **2** skeins of floss.

★ Use long stitches.

° Use **DMC 520** for letters G and O. Use **DMC 676** for letters D, J, T, and Z. Use **DMC 729** for letters C, I, S, and Y. Use **DMC 760** for letters F, N, and V. Use **DMC 927** for letters B, L, R, and X. Use **DMC 3052** for letters H and P. Use **DMC 3328** for letters E, M, and U. Use **DMC 3768** for letters A, K, Q, and W.

Note: To personalize, use alphabet and numbers provided. Make each Eyelet Stitch a Cross Stitch using 2 strands of floss over two fabric threads.

Stitch Count (241w x 221h)

14 count	17 1/4" x 15 7/8"
16 count	15 1/8" x 13 7/8"
18 count	13 1/2" x 12 3/8"

Chart sections are on pgs. 80-85.
Detail charts are on pg. 91.
See Placement Diagram on pg. 83.

Section 1

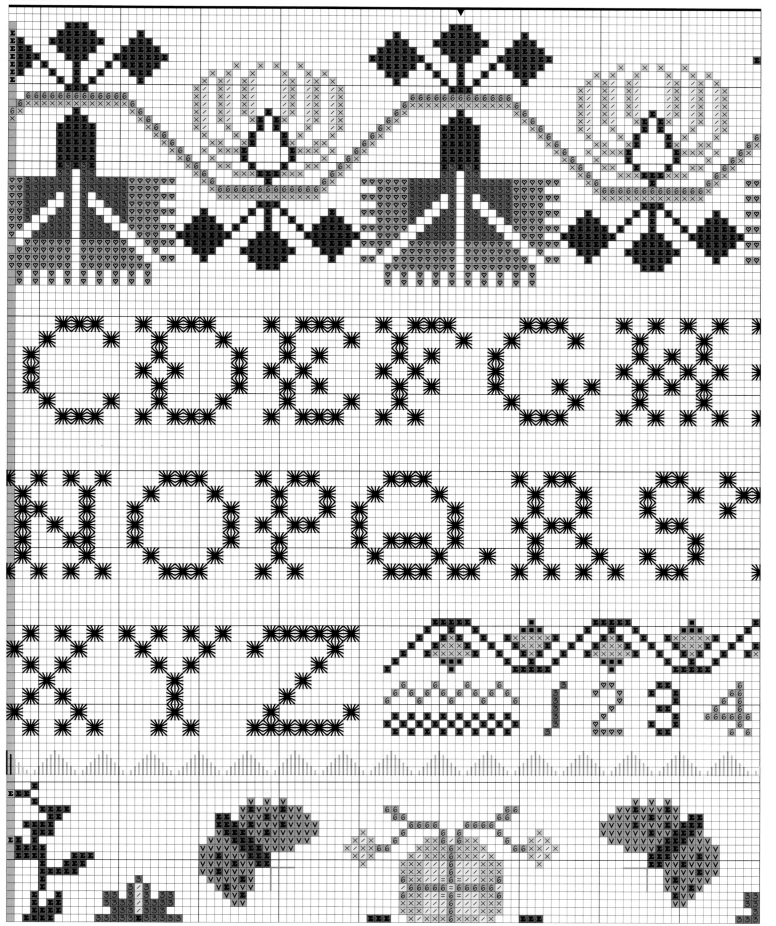

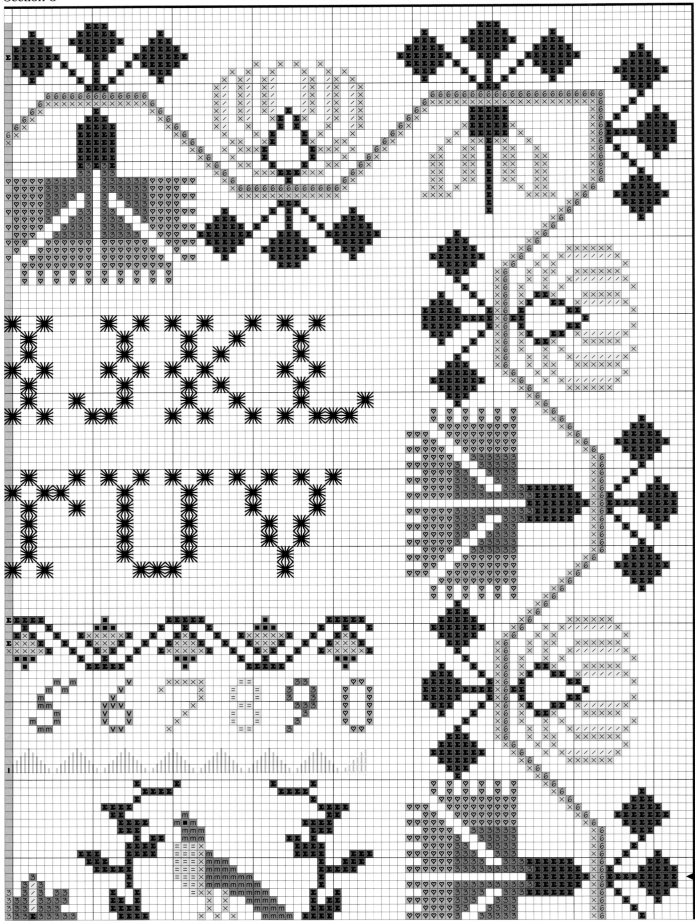

FLORA SAMPLER

X	DMC	B'ST	ANC.
Σ	*520	╱★	862
=	676		891
╱	677		886
✕	†729		890
♡	†760		1022
■	839		1086
✳	840		1084
V	927		848
6	†3052	╱	262
3	†3328		1024
m	†3768		779

	DMC	STITCH
✳°		Eyelet Stitch, pg. 96
	3052	Satin Stitch, pg. 96
	3328	Plait Stitch, pg. 96
	3768	Rice Stitch, pg. 96
		Grey area indicates last row of previous section of design.

* You will need **3** skeins of floss.

† You will need **2** skeins of floss.

★ Use long stitches.

° Use **DMC 520** for letters G and O. Use **DMC 676** for letters D, J, T, and Z. Use **DMC 729** for letters C, I, S, and Y. Use **DMC 760** for letters F, N, and V. Use **DMC 927** for letters B, L, R, and X. Use **DMC 3052** for letters H and P. Use **DMC 3328** for letters E, M, and U. Use **DMC 3768** for letters A, K, Q, and W.

Design was stitched on a $21^1/_2$" x 20" piece of 32 count Cream Belfast Linen (design size $15^1/_8$" x $13^7/_8$") over two fabric threads. Two strands of floss were used for Cross Stitch, Specialty Stitches, and Backstitch. One strand of floss was used for Cross Stitch over one fabric thread. It was custom framed.

Placement Diagram

Section 1	Section 2	Section 3
Section 4	Section 5	Section 6

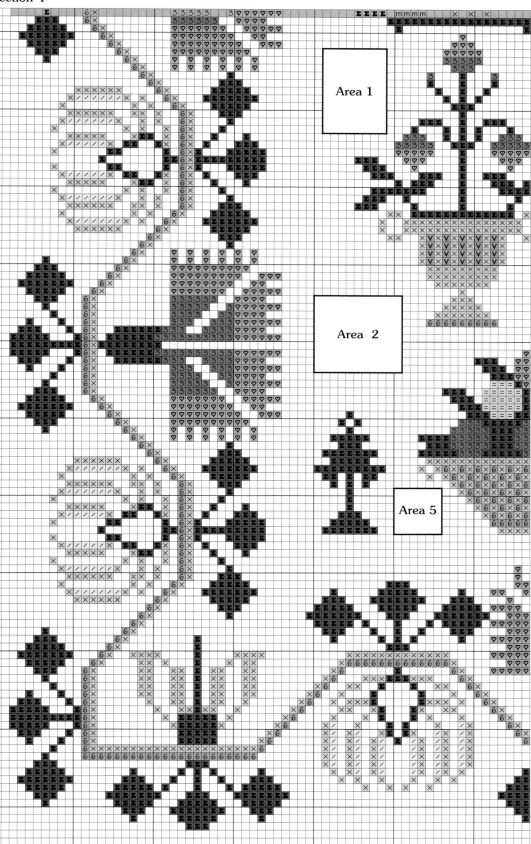

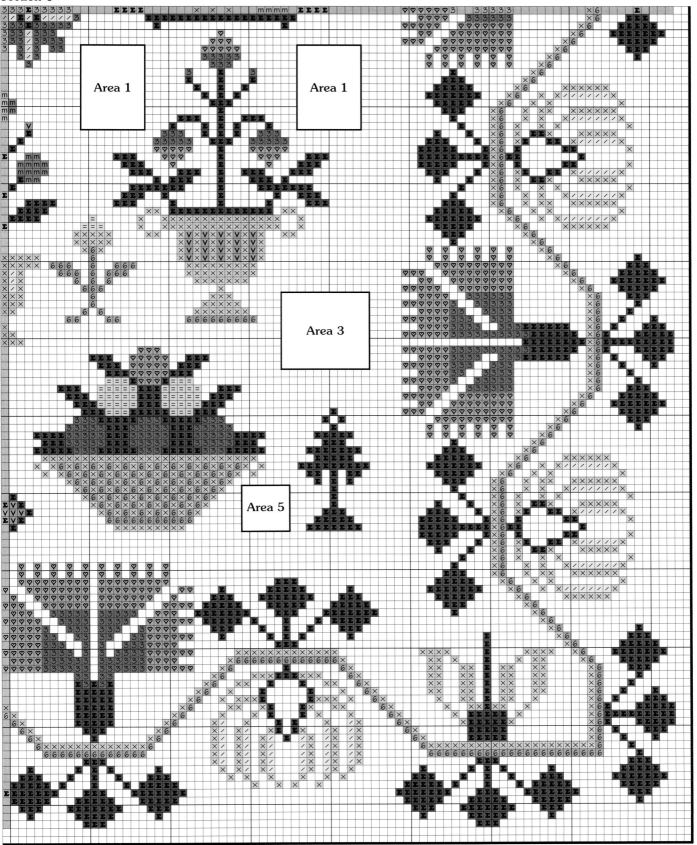

REMEMBER ME SAMPLER

X	DMC	ANC.
3	355	1014
↑	356	5975
⊖	422	943
✓	646	8581
★	677	886
✳	*936	269
2	3052	262
N	3768	779

	DMC	Stitch
▢	356	Four-sided Stitch, pg. 96
☰	936	Satin Stitch, pg. 96
☰	3052	Satin Stitch, pg. 96
✳	3052	Algerian Eyelet Stitch, pg. 96
▢	3768	Montenegrin Stitch, pg. 96
▢	Grey area indicates last row of previous section of design.	

* You will need **2** skeins of floss.

Section 1

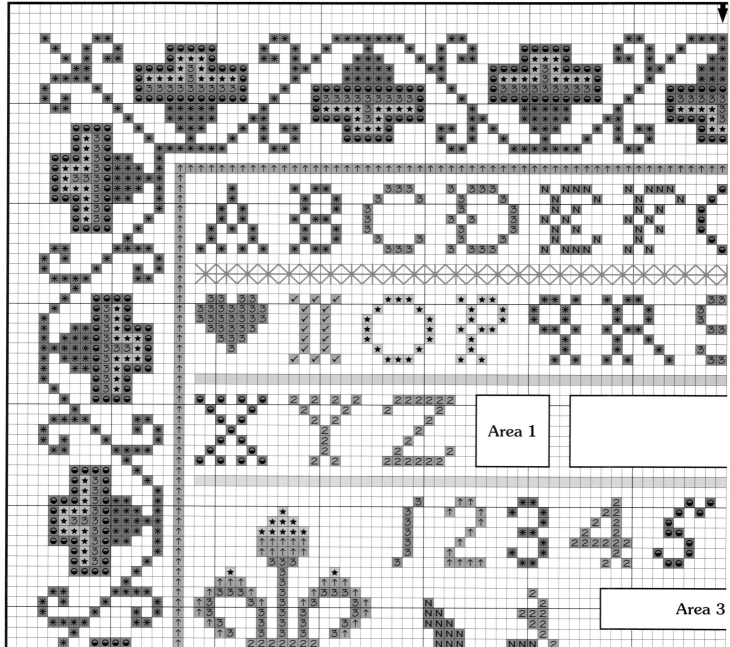

Design was stitched on a 15½" x 15½" piece of 28 count Cream Cashel Linen® (design size 9⅜" x 9⅜") over two fabric threads. Two strands of floss were used for Cross Stitch and Specialty Stitches. One strand of floss was used for Cross Stitch over one fabric thread. It was custom framed.

Note: To personalize, use alphabet and numbers provided.

Stitch Count (131w x 131h)
14 count   9⅜"   x   9⅜"
16 count   8¼"   x   8¼"
18 count   7⅜"   x   7⅜"

Chart sections are on pgs. 86-89.
Detail charts are on pgs. 90-91.
See placement diagram below.

Section 1	Section 2
Section 3	Section 4

Section 2

Area 2

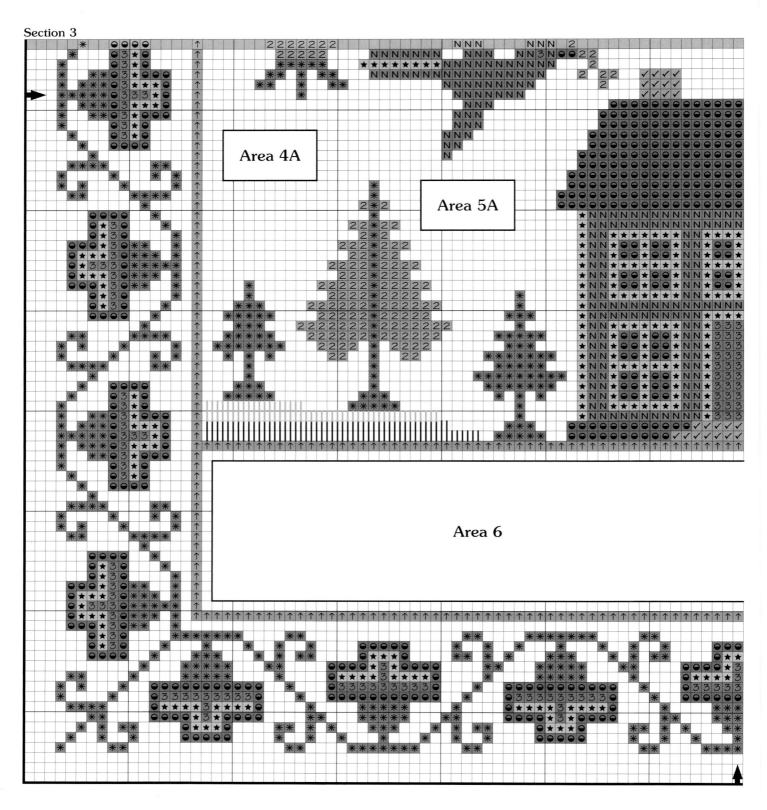

Area 4A

Area 5A

Area 6

REMEMBER ME SAMPLER

X	DMC	ANC.
3	355	1014
↑	356	5975
◖	422	943
✓	646	8581
★	677	886

X	DMC	ANC.
✳*	936	269
2	3052	262
N	3768	779
		Grey area indicates last row
		of previous section of design.

	DMC	Stitch
	356	Four-sided Stitch, pg. 96
▥	936	Satin Stitch, pg. 96
▥	3052	Satin Stitch, pg. 96
✳	3052	Algerian Eyelet Stitch, pg. 96
	3768	Montenegrin Stitch, pg. 96

* You will need **2** skeins
of floss.

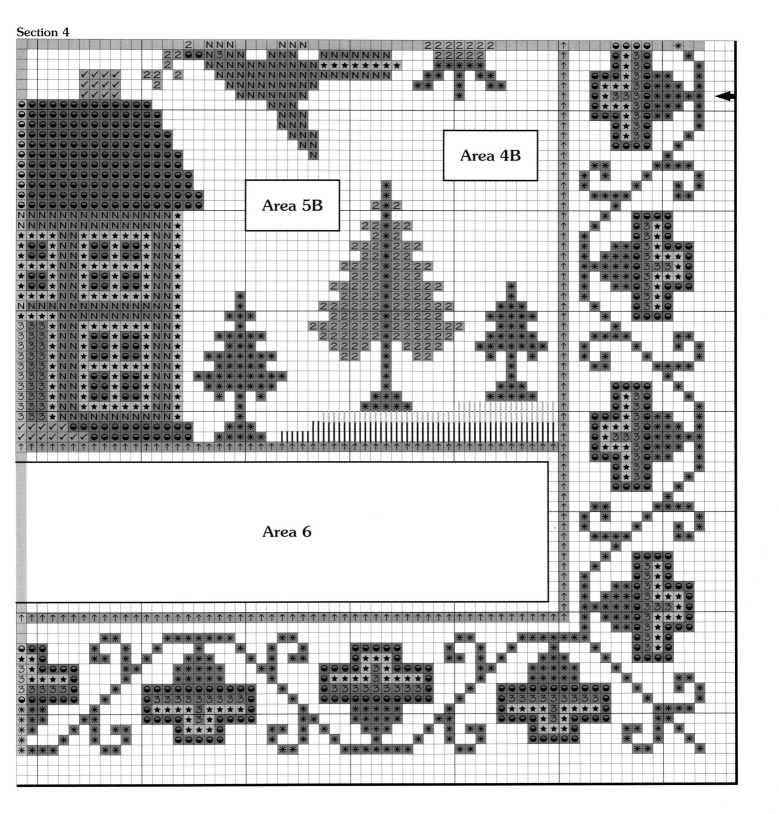

Area 4B

Area 5B

Area 6

Detail Charts
Remember Me Sampler
(Worked over one fabric thread)

Note: Heavy line is for placement only. Do not stitch.

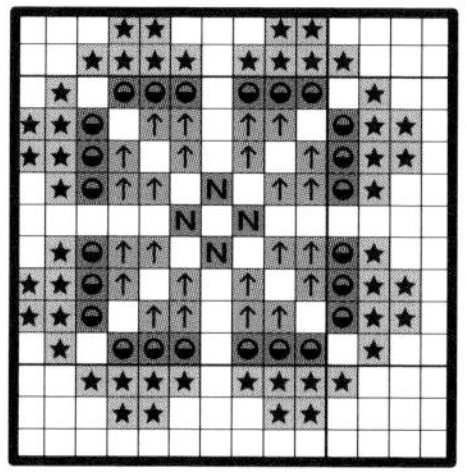

Area 1

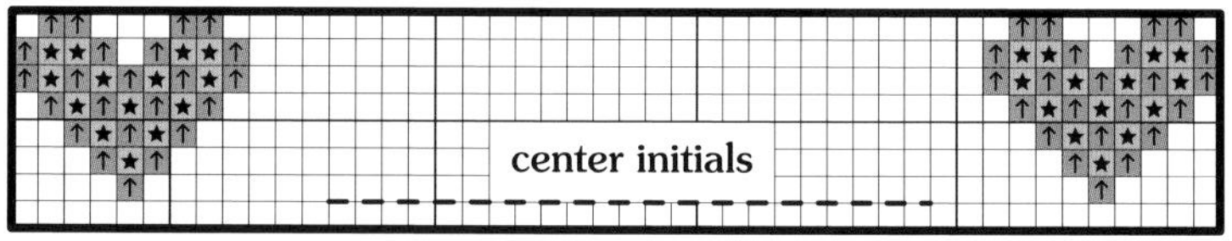

Area 3

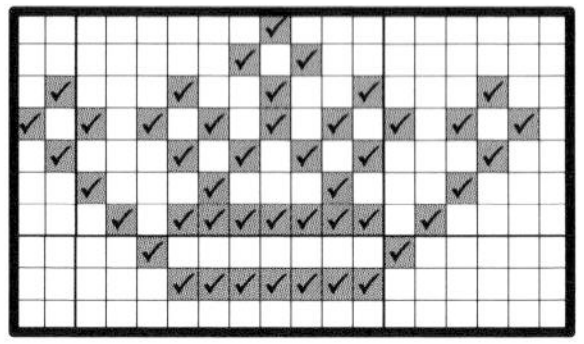

center initials

Area 2

Area 4A

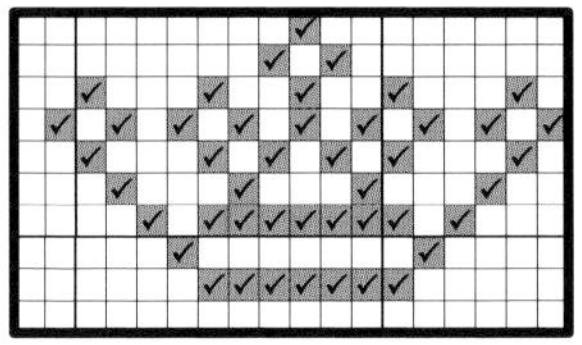

Area 4B

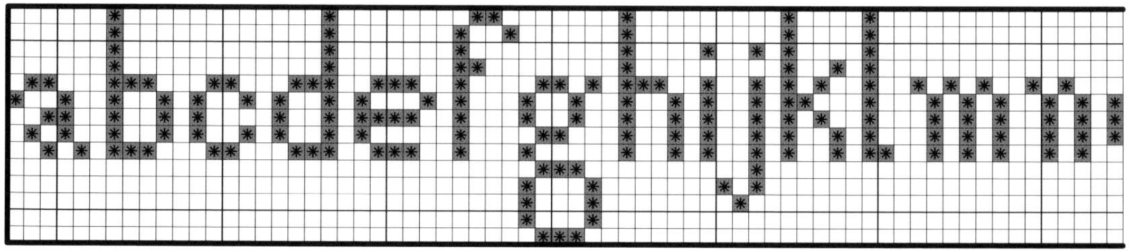

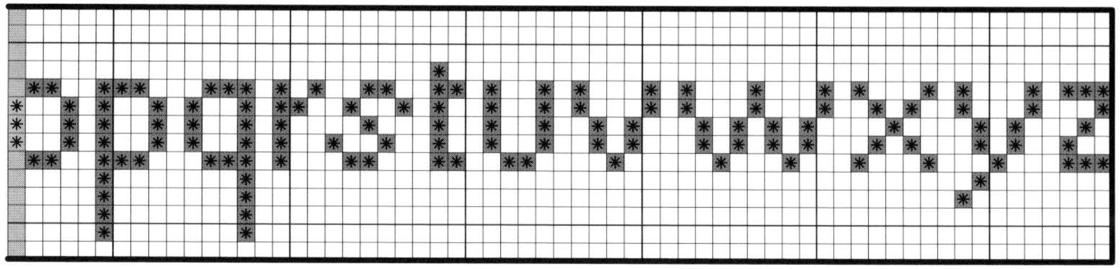

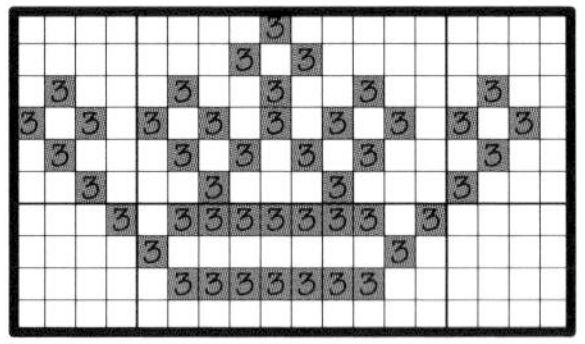

Area 5A

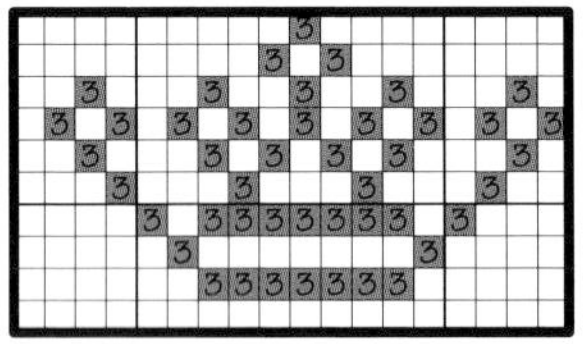

Area 5B

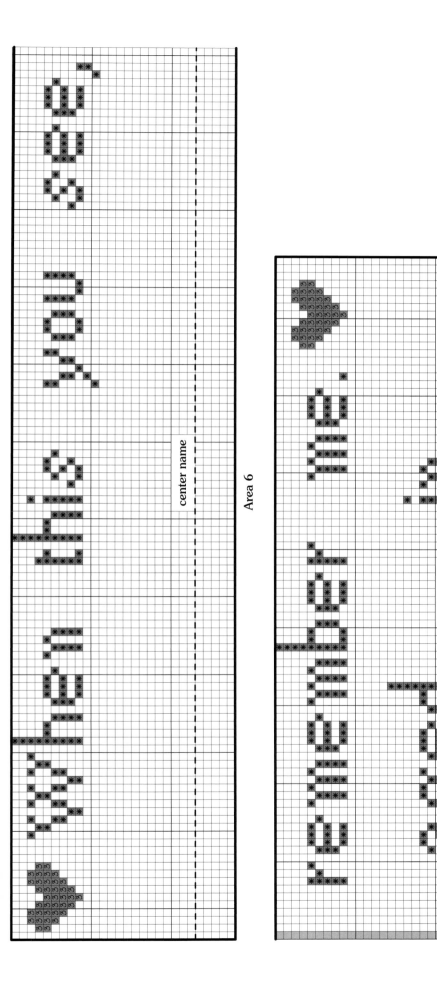

Area 6

center name

center year

center age

Detail Charts
Flora Sampler
(Worked over one fabric thread)

Note: Heavy line is for placement only. Do not stitch.

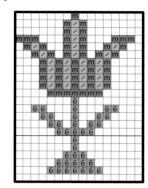

Area 1

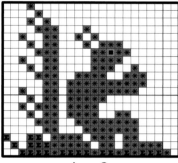

Area 2

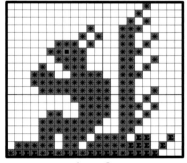

Area 3

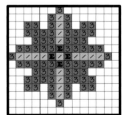

Area 4

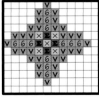

Area 5

91

X	DMC	¼X	B'ST	ANC.
☆	blanc	▱	╱★	2
L	*blanc & 437	L		2 & 362
√	*blanc & 640	√		2 & 903
○	*blanc & 746			2 & 275
▼	*blanc & 3021	▼		2 & 905
✳	*300 & 3790			352 & 393
Z	*301 & 640			1049 & 903
)	310	◢	╱+	403
¢	*310 & 3371	¢		403 & 382
↑	*433 & 975	↑		358 & 355
e	*434 & 976	e		310 & 1001
	435		╱+	1046
=	*435 & 977	=		1046 & 1002
>	437			362
×	640	×		903
	642		╱★	392
∩	*642 & 644	∩		392 & 830
‖	645			273
T	646	T		8581
−	*676 & 729	−		891 & 890
C	*676 & 746	c		891 & 275
a	*676 & 3782			891 & 899
	729		╱★	890
4	*729 & 976	4		890 & 1001
m	*729 & 3032	m		890 & 903
⊥	742	⊥		303
H	*742 & 977	H		303 & 1002
◊	743	◊		302
+	*745 & 3782			300 & 899
V	*746 & 3033			275 & 391

X	DMC	¼X	B'ST	ANC.
	844		╱	1041
⊖	*844 & 3371	⊖		1041 & 382
	935		╱†	861
	937		╱†	268
L	*938 & 3021	L		381 & 905
8	976	8	╱★	1001
	3012		╱†	844
	3021		╱	905
◇	3023	◇		1040
n	*3032 & 3790	n		903 & 393
3	*3033 & 3782			391 & 899
△	3371	△	╱+	382
5	3787	5		273
6	3790	6		393
●	blanc Fr. Knot			2
▦	Grey area indicates last row of previous section of design.			

* Use **1** strand of each floss color listed.
† Use long stitches and randomly place colors when stitching pine needles.

★ **DMC blanc** for wings and bottom of right owl's foot. **DMC 642** for tails. **DMC 729** for left owl's foot. **DMC 976** for top of right owl's foot.

+ **DMC 310** for eyes (use **2** strands for outer edge of eye), beaks, and talons. **DMC 435** for left owl's chest. **DMC 3371** for left owl's foot.

Design was stitched on a 16" x 12½" piece of 28 count Olive Green Cashel Linen® (design size 10" x 6½") over two fabric threads. Two strands of floss were used for Cross Stitch and French Knots and 1 strand for Backstitch except where noted in key. It was custom framed.

Stitch Count (140w x 90h)

14 count	10"	x 6½"
16 count	8¾"	x 5⅝"
18 count	7⅞"	x 5"

Charts are on pgs. 92-94.
See Placement Diagram on pg. 94.

SAW-WHET OWLS

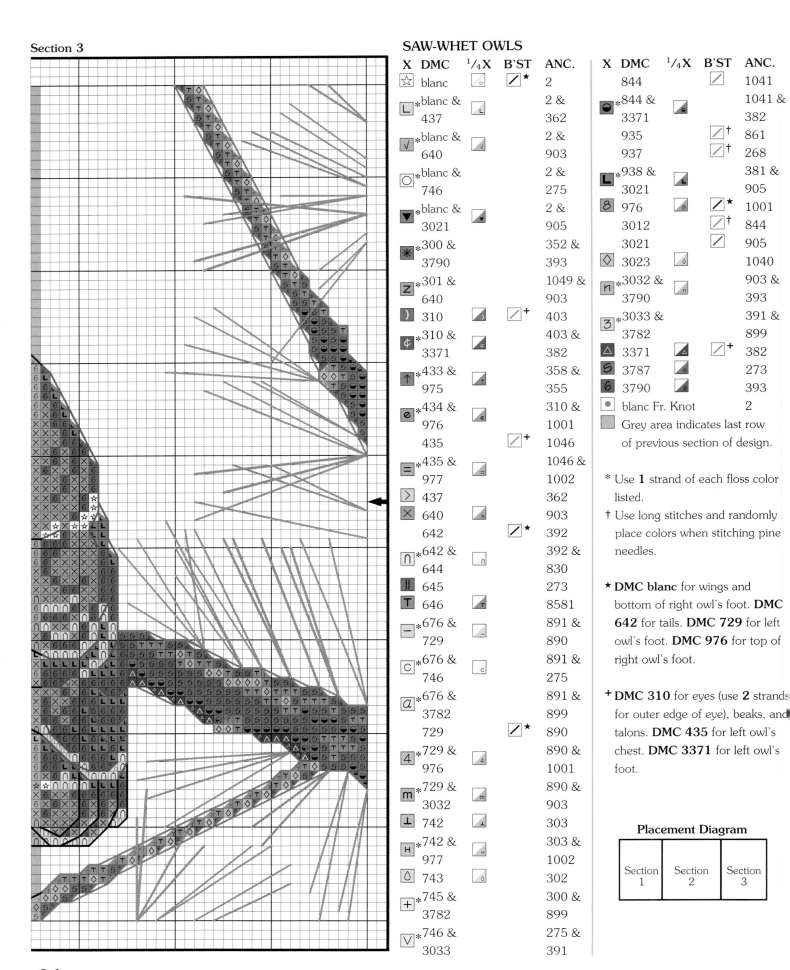

X	DMC	1/4X	B'ST	ANC.
☆	blanc		/★	2
L	*blanc & 437			2 & 362
√	*blanc & 640			2 & 903
○	*blanc & 746			2 & 275
▼	*blanc & 3021			2 & 905
✱	300 & 3790			352 & 393
Z	*301 & 640			1049 & 903
)	310		/+	403
¢	310 & 3371			403 & 382
↑	*433 & 975			358 & 355
e	*434 & 976			310 & 1001
	435		/+	1046
=	*435 & 977			1046 & 1002
>	437			362
X	640			903
	642		/★	392
∩	*642 & 644			392 & 830
‖	645			273
T	646			8581
−	*676 & 729			891 & 890
C	*676 & 746			891 & 275
a	*676 & 3782			891 & 899
	729		/★	890
4	*729 & 976			890 & 1001
m	*729 & 3032			890 & 903
⊥	742			303
H	*742 & 977			303 & 1002
◊	743			302
+	*745 & 3782			300 & 899
V	*746 & 3033			275 & 391

X	DMC	1/4X	B'ST	ANC.
	844		/	1041
◖	*844 & 3371			1041 & 382
	935		/†	861
	937		/†	268
L	*938 & 3021			381 & 905
8	976		/★	1001
	3012		/†	844
	3021		/	905
◊	3023			1040
n	*3032 & 3790			903 & 393
3	*3033 & 3782			391 & 899
△	3371		/+	382
S	3787			273
6	3790			393
•	blanc Fr. Knot			2

Grey area indicates last row of previous section of design.

* Use **1** strand of each floss color listed.

† Use long stitches and randomly place colors when stitching pine needles.

★ **DMC blanc** for wings and bottom of right owl's foot. **DMC 642** for tails. **DMC 729** for left owl's foot. **DMC 976** for top of right owl's foot.

+ **DMC 310** for eyes (use **2** strands for outer edge of eye), beaks, and talons. **DMC 435** for left owl's chest. **DMC 3371** for left owl's foot.

Placement Diagram

Section 1	Section 2	Section 3

HOW TO READ CHARTS

Each chart is made up of a key and a gridded design where each square represents a stitch. The symbols in the key tell which floss color to use for each stitch in the chart. The following headings and symbols are given:

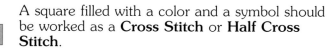 **X** — Cross Stitch
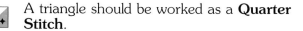 **DMC** — DMC color number
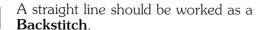 **¹/₄ X** — Quarter Stitch
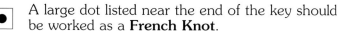 **¹/₂ X** — Half Cross Stitch
B'ST — Backstitch
ANC. — Anchor color number

A square filled with a color and a symbol should be worked as a **Cross Stitch** or **Half Cross Stitch**.

A triangle should be worked as a **Quarter Stitch**.

A straight line should be worked as a **Backstitch**.

A large dot listed near the end of the key should be worked as a **French Knot**.

Sometimes the symbol for a **Cross Stitch** may be partially covered when a **Backstitch** crosses the square. Refer to the background color to determine the floss color.

HOW TO STITCH

Always work **Cross Stitches**, **Quarter Stitches**, and **Half Cross Stitches** first and then add the **Backstitch** and **French Knots**.

Cross Stitch (X): For horizontal rows, work stitches in two journeys *(Fig. 1)*. For vertical rows, complete each stitch as shown *(Fig. 2)*. When working over two fabric threads, work Cross Stitch as shown in **Fig. 3**.

Fig. 1

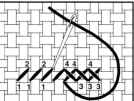

Fig. 2

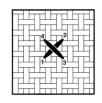

Fig. 3

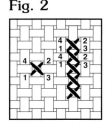

Quarter Stitch (¹/₄X): Come up at 1 *(Fig. 4)*, then split fabric thread to go down at 2. **Fig. 5** shows the technique for Quarter Stitch when working over two fabric threads.

Fig. 4

Fig. 5

Half Cross Stitch (¹/₂X): This stitch is one journey of the Cross Stitch and is worked from lower left to upper right as shown in **Fig. 6**. When working over two fabric threads, work Half Cross Stitch as shown in **Fig. 7**.

Fig. 6

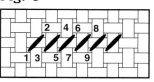

Fig. 7

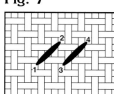

Backstitch (B'ST): For outlines and details, Backstitch should be worked after the design has been completed *(Fig. 8)*. When working over two fabric threads, work Backstitch as shown in **Fig. 9**.

Fig. 8

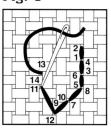

Fig. 9

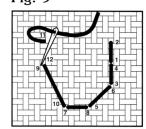

French Knot: Bring needle up at 1. Wrap floss once around needle. Insert needle at 2, tighten knot, and pull needle through fabric, holding floss until it must be released *(Fig. 10)*. For a larger knot, use more floss strands; wrap only once.

Fig. 10

We have made every effort to ensure that these instructions are accurate and complete. We cannot, however, be responsible for human error, typographical mistakes, or variations in individual work.

We would like to recognize Husqvarna Viking Sewing Machine Company of Cleveland, Ohio, for providing the sewing machines used to make some of our projects.

Instructions tested and some photography models made by Phyllis Lundy.

STITCHING TIPS

Preparing Fabric

Being sure to allow plenty of margin, cut fabric desired size and overcast raw edges. It is better to waste a little fabric than to come up short after hours of stitching!

Working with Floss

To ensure smoother stitches, separate strands and realign them before threading needle. Keep stitching tension consistent. Begin and end floss by running under several stitches on back; never tie knots.

Dye Lot Variation

It is important to buy all of the floss you need to complete your project from the same dye lot. Although variations in color may be slight when flosses from two different dye lots are held together, the variation is usually apparent on a stitched piece.

Where to Start

The horizontal and vertical centers of each charted design are shown by arrows. You may start at any point on the charted design, but be sure the design will be centered on the fabric. Locate the center of fabric by folding in half, top to bottom and again left to right. On the charted design, count the number of squares (stitches) from the center of the chart to where you wish to start. Then from the fabric's center, find your starting point by counting out the same number of fabric threads (stitches). *(To work over two fabric threads, count out twice the number of fabric threads.)*

Working over Two Fabric Threads

When working over two fabric threads, the stitches should be placed so that vertical fabric threads support each stitch. Make sure that the first Cross Stitch is placed on the fabric with stitch 1-2 beginning and ending where a vertical fabric thread crosses over a horizontal fabric thread *(Fig. 11)*.

Fig. 11

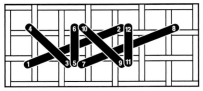

Making a Pillow

When sewing, match right sides and raw edges and use a 1/2" seam allowance.

1. Trim stitched piece to desired finished shape and size plus 1/2" on all sides for seam allowances.
2. Cut one length of purchased trim the same measurement as outer edge of pillow front plus 1".
3. Beginning at one end, baste trim to pillow front along seam line; overlap beginning end.
4. Cut a piece of backing fabric same size as pillow front. Sew front to back, leaving an opening at bottom edge. Trim corners diagonally, turn right side out, and press. Stuff with polyester fiberfill; slipstitch opening closed.

Montenegrin Stitch

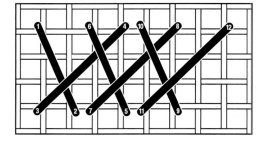

Cross Stitch
(over 1 fabric thread)

When working over one fabric thread on linen, do not pull floss too tight. This may cause stitches to be drawn behind fabric threads.

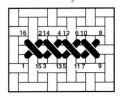

Rice Stitch

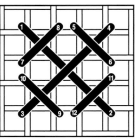

Eyelet Stitch

Algerian Eyelet Stitch

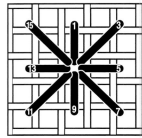

Satin Stitch

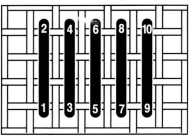

Four-sided Stitch

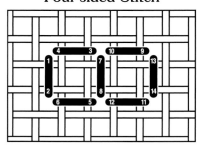

Plait Stitch